The Writer Who Inhabits Your Body

"Gregorio explores the relationship between the human body and creativity in a way that will benefit all writers. In this book you'll find thoughtful insight, encouragement, and dynamic exercises. Gregorio's approach can both inspire the beginner and help practicing writers deepen and expand. *The Writer Who Inhabits Your Body* is both a friend and teacher. Follow along!"

MIRIAM SAGAN, AUTHOR OF
UNBROKEN LINE: WRITING IN THE LINEAGE OF POETRY

"This is a wonderful resource for anyone who writes or has ever wanted to write. Using practices and principles from aikido, Renée offers exercises that awaken the mind/body/spirit connection, activating inspiration and insights from a place 'rich with untapped knowing.' She invites readers to open heart and soul and shows how to tap the creativity that emerges from their internal landscape."

WENDY PALMER, AUTHOR OF
LEADERSHIP EMBODIMENT AND *DRAGONS AND POWER*

"A wonderfully crafted, beautifully written, highly accessible approach that illuminates and takes you through the doorway of writing. Gregorio takes you on a journey into your heart, gut, and embodied soul that sparkles with revelations in how your dreams, images, and longings become language."

RICHARD STROZZI-HECKLER, AUTHOR OF
EMBODYING THE MYSTERY

"A writing process that is so much more than words on paper with pen or ink. Your words will spill, erupt, fly, and whisper, emergent foremost from who you are yourself. Gregorio will help you bring yourself to the page. Get quiet and listen to your own voice."

NANCY SHANTEAU, COOPERATIVE COMMUNICATION
TEACHER AND COACH

"In *The Writer Who Inhabits Your Body*, Renée speaks powerfully to the benefits of the ongoing process of settling and clearing, which brings about wider and wider rings of listening, until the writer and what's being written about are in harmonious relationship."

ROBERT NADEAU, 8TH DEGREE BLACK BELT,
AIKIDO MASTER

"What an honor to explore writing as path, aikido as path, somatics as path, with someone who has been in practice for decades. This book is an invitation to the interface of what is most internal and the offering of that to the world. Scary and full of awe."

STACI K. HAINES, SOMATIC TEACHER AND
AUTHOR OF *THE POLITICS OF TRAUMA*

"Provides pathways of understanding and profound practices to guide writers into themselves with all the complexities, challenges, and opportunities writers face. In this way, Gregorio leaves no stone unturned and provides practical hope to being a writer. A masterful work."

SUZANNE ROBERTS, PRINCIPAL OF UNIFYINGSOLUTIONS
OF ANTI-RACISM COLLECTIVE,
POLARITY THERAPY TEACHER, AND COACH

"In this exquisite book of heart and feeling, wisdom and practice, Renée Gregorio deftly guides the reader through practices that plumb the depths of that stream. This book is a must-read for anyone who is longing for 'a place where you know what it means to rest in yourself and let words arise.'"

CHRIS L. JOHNSON, PSYD., FOUNDER OF Q4 CONSULTING
AND AUTHOR OF *THE LEADERSHIP PAUSE*

"This book is a gift: a poetic, embodied, and practical guide that lets you spring forth as written word."

GINNY WHITELAW, AUTHOR OF
RESONATE AND *THE ZEN LEADER*

The Writer Who Inhabits Your Body

Somatic Practices to Enhance Creativity and Inspiration

Renée Gregorio

Park Street Press
Rochester, Vermont

Park Street Press
One Park Street
Rochester, Vermont 05767
www.ParkStPress.com

Park Street Press is a division of Inner Traditions International

Cataloging-in-Publication Data for this title is available from the Library of Congress

ISBN 978-1-64411-923-5 (print)
ISBN 978-1-64411-924-2 (ebook)

Printed and bound in the United States by Lake Book Manufacturing, LLC
The text stock is SFI certified. The Sustainable Forestry Initiative® program promotes sustainable forest management.

10 9 8 7 6 5 4 3 2 1

Text design and layout by Priscilla Harris Baker
This book was typeset in Garamond Premier Pro with Futura, Gill Sans, Museo Sans, Rosarian, and Ten Oldstyle used as display typefaces
Illustrations by Jacquie Bellon
Author photo (page 173) by Julie Claire

To send correspondence to the author of this book, mail a first-class letter to the author c/o Inner Traditions • Bear & Company, One Park Street, Rochester, VT 05767, and we will forward the communication, or contact the author directly at **ReneeGregorio.com**.

Aiki

This is the beginning place, the place the cup
gets emptied and I am bare
as blank page,
layers peeled away,
onion finding its fleshy center.
It could make me cry here, such openings
finding voice, finding spirit underneath spirit.
Or I could laugh here over something partially
obscene, partially hidden. I could laugh here
at the difference between erratic and erotic,
at the ways I'm thrown. Or my head could get turned
in several directions at once, showing the way I hold on too tightly,
the way one energy can shut me down, shut me up,
while another makes me want to sing loudly and off-key.
This is the place body finds her voice—
as good as coffee ice cream and bumper cars,
kid at a carnival,
as ready as a fresh wound
for new skin to emerge.

FROM GREGORIO, THE STORM THAT TAMES US

Contents

Part One
Center Is Everything

Part Four

The Roar of Your Writing

Words That Become You

The Writer Who Inhabits Your Body is not a book on how to write. It's a book about how to bring heart, body, and soul to your writing. It's a book that will help you come into a stronger relationship with your essential self so that you can write from that place within you—a place where you know what it means to rest in yourself and let words arise. Language born from such a place resonates within all of us and ripples out into the world, touching all of us.

This book will help you to come into relationship with that elusive partner called writing. How do you come into right relationship with yourself first so that the words you really want to write or even to say come tumbling out of you? Who we are as human beings and who we are as crafters of language are inextricably linked. This book will help you to dig deep and find the true language that resides within you. It will help you embody that language and find words that beat to your own pulse—words that matter, words that become you.

Author, speaker, coach, and consultant Richard Strozzi-Heckler wrote that "language is a bodily phenomena and not the result of a dis-embodied mind."[1] Indeed, language arises as much—or more—from our guts and hearts as from our skulls. For language to be powerful, it must arise as much from our bodies as from our minds. How do we know what we know? The way we think, the stories we tell, the poems we write derive from our nervous system, the wisdom of our lived experience, our emotional lives, who we are in mind and body and spirit.

Remember what the poet Rainer Maria Rilke said in *The Notebooks of Malte Laurids Brigge:* that we must see many cities, experience gestures of animals, travel roads in regions we don't know, be beside the dying, have memories of many nights of love. But Rilke also said that memories are not enough: "only when they have changed into our very blood, into glance and gesture" can words truly arise.[2]

Although Rilke did not name it so, this is embodiment. We know what we know and can translate this into language when the knowing, the experience, the sensations, and the emotions have seeped through every fiber of our being and arrived at the tips of our pens.

What does it mean to embody language? It means to come to the conversation, the writing desk, the presentation, the speech with such alignment in yourself that your words take shape from that solid ground, that you feel yourself enough to be able to feel the other, that when the words emerge, they sparkle, they rumble, they beat to your own pulse and to the heartbeat of all you come in contact with.

Have you known what it's like to find your way inside yourself through a body-centered practice such as yoga or a martial art or walking, running, or swimming, perhaps? Such practices can bring us to a place of openness where we tap into the deep stream of what it feels like to be fully alive and to let life flow through us. This life includes energy as well as language. Recently, I returned from a yoga class with a teacher I love because she teaches us to go deeply within ourselves and to move and breathe from a place that is ours alone. I enter such a deep stream through my body as I practice under her guidance. I feel utterly open. Oftentimes, I sense that words want to find their way through this openness, as if such openness is a doorway to language.

This is where the purest stream lives. Our task is to keep finding ways to return to that stream. Of course, getting to that pure stream is not instantaneous. Many teachers have helped me find my stream. Many years of practice have helped me hone my questions. Years of training on the aikido mats have put me in touch with parts of myself

I could not see through language and emotion alone. By moving beside, with, and across from other bodies under the gaze of many powerful teachers, I have felt, witnessed, and shifted parts of my own psyche that I didn't even realize existed. Through the rigor of showing up day after day and year after year on those mats, I could feel, see, and understand the relationship between my psyche and my body and how each could inform the other.

Aikido teachers showed me the importance of centering and gave me practices that would help me deepen that center. Sometimes they gave me this in language. Sometimes they gave me this by example—watching their deeply centered movement and what became possible there. This included moving and blending with another's energy to change the course of an encounter or relationship by engaging with that energy. The importance of alignment—that it's possible to shift perspective and access to our knowing by aligning our energy centers of head, heart, and *hara*—became crucial, as well as the experience and increased ability of shifting even in the moment of consternation or challenge.

I have come to see that center is everything. What began on the aikido mats got amplified through years of study in somatics, leadership, body-centered learning, and coaching. Engaging deeply beside another in the coaching relationship effects change, and placing body-centered learning beside language helps us to trust the knowing that arrives from our guts and hearts as much as from our skulls. We can then see how deeply this affects what we write.

I've worked as a poet for most of my adult life—nearly forty years now—and books of my poems have been published consistently over these decades. Many have been single volumes of my work and several others collaborations with other poets. Over the years, I've often taught workshops privately and in university settings. Sometimes these workshops have centered on poetry writing and other times on a combination of writing practices and body-centered learning. I practiced the martial art aikido for twenty years and earned the rank of *sandan*. For many years I taught aikido at the dojo I attended and also started a small dojo in my community. Aikido led me into the study of somatics where

I earned certification as a master somatic coach. Over the past fifteen years I've worked with hundreds of clients individually. I started teaching body-centered learning beside writing over twenty years ago and have taught, mentored, and coached hundreds of writers and would-be writers.

This book is about bringing this learning to others on the path. It is a path of self-acceptance as much as one of self-discovery. It's a path that leads you to a sense of belonging as much as a sense of belief in the sound of your own voice. Reading these pages and engaging in new practices will help you to find language for your most deeply felt emotions, to own a voice that resonates, to feel words powerfully emerge, and to feel yourself open to language as much as you open to life.

Acknowledgments

*T*here are so many people to thank in the writing of any book. Writing this book came from my desire to integrate decades' worth of training and expertise in three arenas: poetry, aikido, and somatic coaching. First, then, I want to thank the founder of aikido, Morihei Ueshiba, for his art of peace, which has influenced my life and writing in ways I could never have imagined. I take deep bows to my teachers in the art of aikido here in New Mexico: Craig Dunn, Takashi Tokunaga, and Wolfgang Baumgartner. And I turn to those teachers in California who deeply affected my learning by their ability to take aikido "off the mat," to help all of us deepen in our understanding of what the founder meant when he said that aikido helps us polish our spirits. Early on in my training, Robert Nadeau, in particular, opened my eyes, mind, and heart to the "more" of aikido; Wendy Palmer helped me be more consciously embodied; and Richard Strozzi-Heckler, through his Strozzi Institute, challenged me to deepen in my embodiment and, along with Staci Haines, taught me how to help others open to the stream of their lives. Although I have not managed to train (yet) with her directly, Ginny Whitelaw has been an important teacher, too, through her books, presence, and Institute of Zen Leadership. Joy Nagle's Soulfire Yoga classes have been part of my practice for many years now—her presence and light are a necessity! The writing of this book would not have occurred without the facing-into that each of these teachers provided me.

I thank my training partners along these paths, in the aikido dojos and in these learning centers, in particular my colleagues at Strozzi Institute and Presence-Based Coaching. Where would I be without the depth of conversation I am lucky enough to have with Amanda Blake, Chris Johnson, Doug Silsbee, Nancy Shanteau, Suzanne Roberts, Robyn McCullough, Natalia Rabin, and Jackie Crispin Brown? Many of the stories in this book derive from client conversations; I acknowledge the many wonderful clients whom I've learned so much from and who have shaped and informed my work.

Many colleagues reviewed chapters of this book during its making, and I particularly thank my Presence-Based Coaching mastermind group: Tom Hardison, Christine Geithner, Marilyn Woodard, and Kim Ewell, who not only jumped in and provided great feedback on the writing, but who also keep me sane with our monthly conversations. I also thank Debbi Flittner for reviewing chapters and for being my dear friend. I acknowledge the importance of my conversations with Molly Luffy, who is always at the ready to dive deeply with me, to help me see clearly, and to help me dare. The thirty-year correspondence in handwritten letters that Marsha Skinner and I have deeply informs this book. I thank Marsha for her insights, which I could not live without, for being the artist she is in everything she does, and for helping me unearth this thing we call center by being so willing to experiment in her own life and report back to me. I particularly thank a few other dear ones who reviewed my writing but who also listen, go on writing retreats, and exchange stories with me about our lives—Johanna Wald, Barbara Mayfield, and Julie Claire. I thank Natalie Goldberg for her friendship and wisdom regarding the writing life and for putting me in touch with Scott Edelstein, whose assistance and experience provided me with a way forward and ballast when I most needed it. I thank Ed and Jo Ann for their practical and spirited advice and support. And I thank the artist Jacquie Bellon for her exquisite drawings.

Finally, I utterly acknowledge that it's the closest-in ones who help us shape our writing lives. I thank John for all our years of being beside each other as we dive into our own writing, read to each other, provide solid criticism, and hold each other with both rigor and gentleness. This book wouldn't have come forth without what we've made together or without our home as base and as inspiration. Thank you, again. And of course, I thank my mother, Janet, who is always rooting for me and always wise. Deep thanks to my godmother, June, whose wisdom and support are unbounded. Finally, I thank my brother, Paul, for his honesty, courage, intelligence, and humor, which inspire me no end.

As this book becomes a reality, I want to thank those at Inner Traditions who have helped make this so, especially Jon Graham, Kelly Bowen, Manzanita Carpenter, Courtney Jenkins, Jeanie Levitan, Erica Robinson, Katherine Mueller, Ashley Kolesnik, John Hays, and Jamaica Burns—keen eyes and good hearts abounding!

Please Remove Your Shoes

*A*s you enter an aikido dojo, you are asked to remove your shoes before stepping onto the mats. I recall one dojo where the sign read: "Leave your ego with your shoes." The act of removing your shoes has both intimacy and recognition in it—the intimacy of your bare feet touching the mats as you practice and the recognition that you are in new territory, one in which you don't need either your ego or your shoes. The effect is immediately humbling, but also has the seeds of revelation in it. We show up as we are at the doorway, take our shoes off, bow, and enter the space. As we cross that threshold, we leave the events of the day, indeed the world, behind us so that we can fully enter and see what wants to be revealed.

A dojo is a training space, a place of learning, even a place of awakening. In a sense, a dojo is a declared space, an intentional space. We know that when we cross that threshold, something new will occur. We don't know what that is, but as we bow and enter, we are committing to the possibility of learning something new about ourselves, or of putting ourselves on the line, or of being able to feel what it means to blend with another person's energy, or even to be thrown hard by our sensei.

When I left the aikido dojo and the physical training that I'd been committed to for decades, what I missed most was the dojo itself, the sacred space I'd found there and the learning that became possible in that declared space. I kept asking: *Where's my dojo?* I missed the clarity and spirit. And yet I also remembered that I've always thought of the mats as a blank page. So why couldn't I create my own dojo wherever I went and certainly in my writing space? And why can't this very book be a dojo?

So welcome to this shared space we'll occupy together. In the dojo of this book, you'll grapple with and consider many writing-related topics, and you'll encounter and learn from body-centered practices. Through full engagement with the topics and practices presented, you will experience firsthand what it's like to move from constriction to freedom, from a tight heart to an open heart, from silence to speech, from hesitancy to flow.

In an early draft of the manuscript, each chapter began with a poem from one of my books. In reviewing and including this work, I realized again how many of my poems encompass the body, either overtly or energetically. My intent in beginning each chapter with a poem was to give the reader an energetic way into each topic. In the end this seemed a bit cumbersome. But if this idea intrigues you, I encourage you to seek out poems and to let poetry inform you as you move through this book. Let poems fill the spaces around you and within you. Let yourself be touched.

Through this book and through your own words, you'll find your own way forward. The path you'll be on includes the following:

- exploration and deepening of your creative presence
- an increase in your ability to dig deeply within yourself to bring to light what most wants to be expressed
- facing your fears and doubts so you can turn obstacles into doorways
- learning what is central to you, what is uniquely your voice, how to open the portal to that voice
- persisting in expressing what is true for you by honing your original thoughts into more powerful expression

- knowing you're ready to deliver your words with full presence and heart, directness, and confidence

In each chapter you will be presented with the opportunity to try a new practice. The practices are designed to help you experience the topic at hand through your body and through language. I'd encourage you to engage fully with the practices. Get a notebook that's reserved just for your writing and observations as you chart your path, trying out new ways of being and of writing.

When we're given the chance to see and sense ourselves anew through the language of our bodies—which includes our history, commitments, dignity, wounds, moods, identity, strengths, dreams, images, sensations—we expand what we know ourselves to be capable of and we become the powerful voice that is our birthright. Welcome to the dojo!

Part One

Center Is Everything

► Explore what opens up when you build awareness of the physical center of your body and how this increased awareness can be a source for you in your writing.

► Learn about increasing your perceptive abilities through the language of your senses as well as through your center.

► Feel what it means to consciously align energy centers to draw on all of your intelligence.

► Explore what centeredness has to do with care and intention and also how being centered carries over into your writing.

► See how practice can transform your writing life, what a difference repetition, attention, movement, and emotional engagement have on how you bring more aliveness to the work at hand and to yourself.

1
A Source of Knowing

$\mathcal{F}$or nearly twenty years I showed up, sometimes daily, on the aikido mats and practiced. We were practicing a martial art, yes. I was learning how to pin and throw and be pinned and thrown. I was flying through the air at times and landing hard on the mats. I was blending with the energy of countless others, learning how to move *around* rather than *against,* how to extend my energy beyond the limits of my physical body, how to wield a wooden sword or staff and throw another person who held a wooden sword or staff. All this. Yet what I was learning most was what it meant to move from the physical center of my body, the *hara*.

My second aikido teacher, Takashi Tokunaga, would suggest that, when we left the dojo, we do *everything* from this center. I remember practicing driving from center, eating from center, walking from center, playing tennis, cooking, cleaning, making love . . . all this from this newfound place in myself. I began immediately to take the lessons of aikido off the mat and into my life.

Hara is much more than physicality. The first time I sensed this "much more" quality, it related directly to my writing. I'd begun the study and practice of aikido only a few months before. I was only beginning to become familiar with this new concept of moving from the center of my body. I was clumsy at it, but the awareness was beginning to take hold. I was struggling with the writing of a new piece, which was evident in that look of consternation, brows scrunched, head bowed in concentration and concern. I was getting nowhere. Then all of a sudden, I felt my attention drop into my belly, as if I suddenly realized that I had the option of holding my attention there. My pen started moving across the page. I realized I was writing from my belly and that I'd never done that before. I felt a physical difference. I could actually feel the energy moving out from my center. I felt this in my body. I knew that whatever I might be grappling with in language, I could bring into my own center and from there find a new way forward.

Feeling hara allows us to find our balance, yes, in our physical body, but also in our lives. Coming into ourselves is the first step toward knowing what we want to say. Then we can begin to know this truth: that living from our physical center balances us emotionally, spiritually, and intellectually at the same time. The belly is a source of knowing. The Japanese have even elevated this concept of hara to an art form: *haragei,* or the art of living through the belly. Haragei holds the belief that our knowing is brought to plenitude through the belly. Belly as source. A kind of birthing.

Haragei is not only an "art of the stomach," but a particular manner of communication, too, one that is both intuitive and somewhat hidden. Haragei speaks to the sixth sense that the martial arts help to develop in us. It's that sense that you know the other person's next move because you feel it. With haragei, the Japanese might say they exchange thoughts and feelings from one belly to another, without words. This sort of communication is implied, nonverbal and subtle. The belly-to-belly quality of the art is the same: we know another through feeling into our own hara and then feeling into theirs. That simple and that profound. Imagine the implications of this for your writing. Imagine that as you develop your ability to tap into your own belly knowing, you increase your ability to not only know and feel yourself, but also to reach out into the kingdoms (human, animal, natural) of this world and know them anew. All good for increasing and deepening our writing territories, right?

Other Japanese expressions that contain the word *hara* speak to the ways in which "having a belly"—knowing what to do and how to act calmly—is quite distinct from living "without a belly," which is not only dishonorable but dysfunctional. To possess hara means one is fully developed as a human being, all accepting and all embracing. Such a person not only speaks with the belly voice, but even thinks with the belly.

Haragei's territory is nonverbal and relies on intuition and silence. What about expanding the concept of haragei into our writing lives? What if feeling into our haras and developing the ability to both settle our energy there as well as move from our centers could generate new language? By engaging with the art of haragei, we can find another way into language that might even be more true, more solid and more grounded than we've ever known. What would happen if we all started thinking from our bellies and speaking with our belly voices?

When we access hara, we literally seat ourselves more deeply in what we are. Seating ourselves in hara settles us and quiets our more frenetic, achieving natures. What we tend to get caught up in—others' opinions, ambition, comparison, worry—melts away, and we are left with only what is in the moment. The expansive, precious moment. From here we are better able to connect with what is emergent—we can allow what wants to *be,* what wants to live through us. Dropping into the place of hara, we're able to forget our smaller self and open into what is always in the world for us to see, feel, and connect with—other humans, animals, new ideas, creative expression, words, the wind, our breath. When we are deeply seated, we have access to what is beyond us, more than us, larger than us: we touch into the universal.

Over and over and to this day, I practice accessing hara because of the difference this still makes in my writing and life. I go outside each morning with my wooden sword and staff to practice a form derived from aikido that helps me to contact what is *more* than myself. What's important is not so much the skill required to execute these moves as my ability to breathe life and feeling into my body and psyche as I move. The practice never fails to remind me that I live on a particular patch of earth in New Mexico—dry as bone, ragged and magnificent—and that the hills and sky that open up in front of and above me give me breath as much as my lungs do. The practice both settles and energizes me. In a sense it sets me straight to encounter the day's work. I learn to trust, over and over, that I am held by the earth and sky, that the river is running beyond the road even if I can't see it, that there's a life force that is always available to me, and that the more I can get out of my own way and listen to hara, to bone, to the spirits in the worlds beyond this one, the more I'll find my way back to the page that feeds me and be able to let words arrive.

 ## *Practice This*
Dropped Attention and Moving from Hara

Learning to pay attention to and move from the center of your physical body, the hara, takes some time. As you practice you will experience the qualities of moving differently as well as the balance this can help you achieve. You will begin to touch this new source of knowing and to seat yourself more deeply in what you are, what you know.

1. Find a place to walk that allows you to step at least twenty paces. Walk across the space as you would normally walk.

2. When you complete the walk, pause and consider where you placed your attention as you walked. Were you looking at the horizon or at your feet? Were you focused inside or outside yourself? What did you feel or notice as you walked in relationship to balance, mood, or sensation?

3. Now drop your attention to about two inches below your navel, in the center of your body, your hara. Put your hand there if it helps you to focus your attention. Take three deep breaths from your hara.

4. Now walk across the same space, but this time move from your hara. Let your belly lead you. Place your full attention in your hara, step by step. Keep returning to hara if you get distracted or off-balance in any way.

5. Now when you complete your trek, ask yourself what you noticed. What difference did it make, if any, to move from hara?

6. Practice moving from hara throughout the course of a whole day. Note anything that shifts for you as you learn how to drop your attention and move from center.

 *Practice This*
Hara Writing

We can learn to shift where we put our attention and then to see what a difference this makes to our writing. Hara can become another intelligence source that deepens your knowing and your writing.

1. Sit down at your writing desk with notebook and pen. Take the time to settle into yourself, feeling yourself seated in your chair, feet planted. Let yourself take several deep breaths, each breath originating from your belly.

2. Whatever you are thinking or feeling, let it be. Take note of what is pulling you toward it or pushing you away. Let it be. Notice where the pushing and pulling is coming from.

3. Now drop your attention into your belly again. Place your hand there. Breathe several more times into your hara.

4. Ask yourself: What do I care about? What matters to me?

5. If you fly up into your head to answer these questions, so be it. Notice what comes to you from the thinking space. Write for five minutes from your head.

6. Take several more settling breaths and ask again: What do I care about? What matters to me? Keep contacting your breath from your belly and placing your awareness in your hara. Write for another five minutes, letting the words come as much as you can from your belly.

7. Jot down a few differences you noticed between writing from your head and then from your hara. Take this awareness forward.

2

Working through the Body—What Body?

*W*hen I tell clients I can help them write by working *through* the body, maybe what they're thinking is that we will do exercises that might help them have a tighter writing core or that might strengthen their wrists for those writing binges. Of course, this is not what I mean. *Body* is so much more than skin and bones, organs and blood. And much of our conditioning tells us that the body is separate from the mind, and that the mind is superior. We have all been trained to rely on our heads much more than our hearts and most certainly more than our guts. We can get into trouble when we separate out *body* from the rest of ourselves—mind, heart, spirit, gut—rather than see ourselves as a unified whole, a living system that's always expressing itself through thoughts, feelings, desires, relationships, ways of being.

What if, instead, our bodies actually held untapped wisdom? What if we could examine and understand that we don't just *have* a body; we *are* a body? The body that we are is a vehicle or vessel that holds and releases life energies—and we each have our own signature on how we do this.

I prefer the word *soma* to *body*. Soma is the living body in its wholeness. It is the intricate way in which who we are in our bodies affects our beliefs, our moods, and our ability to move in our lives or to take

11

particular actions in the world. The body is not divorced from who we are, a separate entity that we lug around that often causes us difficulty, that seems to hurt more as we age. The soma holds our life energies; it's a container for those energies, which are always moving through us—or could be. Our soma is made up of all the ways we hold our experience, of the ways we feel joy, fear, safety, and dignity—a complex mix. Our soma speaks to both our body and the ever-changing nature of how that body is a vehicle for the life that wants to move through it.

If as individuals we are shaped as much by our culture as by our family systems, institutions, and the environment itself, then we are constantly being shaped and reshaped as we move through our lives, as we are affected by personal circumstance alongside political realities, climate change, cultural and societal norms, our own desires and longing. All of this mix is who we are, and who we are is always changing. We are a walking embodiment of all our beliefs formed over our lifetimes, and all those beliefs, habits, and ways of relating cause us to take certain actions in our lives, or not.

The language we are capable of is directly related to who and how we are *somatically*. If our muscles have memory and our tissues are intelligent, it makes sense to work *through* the body to craft language that is powerful and true. The body is a living molecular process, and it's meant to be the vessel for our energies to move through, for life itself to move through. The more we can become an open vessel that accepts those energies and doesn't name them good or bad but rather sees them for themselves, the more we can step aside and let the language that wants to be written come through us onto the page.

One of the first ways to bring awareness to our somatic self is by beginning to know our sensations. In doing so we locate ourselves in the present moment because sensations only exist in the present. We increase our ability to live in the present, to create from the present. Working with *what is* through the language of sensation is a powerful act.

Initially, we might be drawn to the five senses of taste, touch, sight, smell, and hearing. These well-known senses aren't the whole picture, though. The five senses are all a part of what's called *exteroception,* which aids in our perception of the world surrounding us. Another class of sensory information, *interoception*, helps us perceive the world inside ourselves—through the heart, gut, lungs, skin, and connective tissue. The third class of sensory information available to us is called *proprioception*, which helps us sense where our body is in space.

But don't worry too much about these classes of sensory information—just be aware that there's a lot of possibility in terms of what we sense and feel beyond our five senses. Our senses—all of them—can give us useful information and help us tap into the body's wisdom. Of course, it's likely easier to feel into one of those five senses than it is to sense what's up in your connective tissue—but I'd guess that if you ask your heart or gut what it's sensing, there will be an answer. Likewise, you can begin to pay more attention to how your body takes up space, to its sense of balance or imbalance, to the tilt of your head or the way you lean back or forward, depending on the situation you find yourself in. Sensations can lead us into experiencing a particular emotion or fear. I encourage you to engage with the sensation itself, before your interpreting mind activates.

In the chapters that follow you will learn to increase your capacity to live inside your own skin, to feel your sensations, to name what you see and feel. And then to align all that you are, all that you've been, with what you want to create now. To let life move through you freely. To create from this state of flow. To find language that matches who you deeply are.

 ## Practice This
Centering to Build Creative Presence

Centering helps us to be in the present, to feel ourselves wholly, and to increase our ability to perceive the world within and around our physical bodies. Try the following practice, adapted from Strozzi Institute's centering practice.

1. Stand up and keep your eyes open. Place your right hand on your hara, that center point about two inches below your navel. Breathe from there, in and out. Feel yourself from top to bottom—feel the

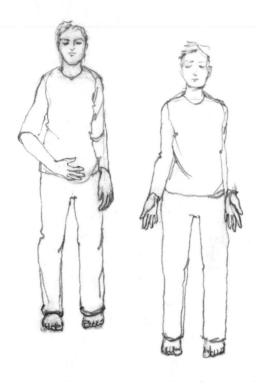

The figure at left shows the hand at the hara; at right the hands drop to the sides of the body.

lift above your head, as if you are being pulled upward, while also feeling your feet on the ground. Let there be space between your vertebrae, along your shoulder blades, and at that tight spot in your lower back.

2. Take a deep breath and let it go. Let your hands drop gently to your sides. Feel your length. Feel how you belong on the earth, right in this spot you are in. Notice how it is to bring spaciousness to your length.

3. While continuing to be in your length, begin to add in the dimension of width. Do this by feeling out to the edges of your skin from the top of your head down your neck, arms, waist, hips, knees, ankles, feet. Notice how you can feel out from your own physical body, to the field to the right and left of you. How far out can you feel? Is one side more readily available to you than the other? Just notice. Can you feel out into the room with your attention and include someone else in that attention while staying in your length, your own sense of belonging and dignity?

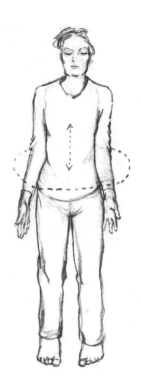

The dimensionality of centering—first feeling the vertical dimension of length in the body (represented here by the vertical arrow), then the dimensions of width to the right and left of the body, and finally depth to the front and back of the body (shown by the dotted circle around the body).

4. Then add in depth. Do this by feeling deep into your blood and bones and organs. Can you feel your heart? Your gut? Then notice the field in front of you. Can you extend your energy into that field? What is that like for you? Now, behind you. What does the field behind you feel like?

5. Now feel all three dimensions simultaneously: length, width, depth. Let yourself extend as fully as you can into each dimension, feeling space and possibility in each. Let your experience be incremental, each building on each, as you feel length, then add in width without losing length, then add in depth without losing length and width.

6. At the heart of feeling yourself wholly now, ask yourself what you most care about in your writing, in your expression, in the way you live your life. Let this sink in. Speak it out loud. *I care deeply about . . .*

7. Take the time to write about your experiences. What happened in each dimension as you practiced this way of centering? Observe where you hold tension or where you have spaciousness available

to you. What do you most care about in terms of your own expression and being?

8. Bring the practice of centering into every day. Center consciously several times a day. You can practice centering while standing, while in your writing space, while sitting, while driving—anywhere, actually.

Now let's try some ways into increasing awareness of your sensations, just as they are, without judgment or explanation.

 ## Practice This
The Language of Sensation

We're so good at living in our heads, thinking our way through whatever arises—let's practice feeling our way instead.

1. Return to the practice of centering that you just did. Now that you've practiced centering once, try it again without the instructions, letting yourself feel deeply into each dimension—length, width, and depth.

2. This time as you practice centering, pay particular attention to your sensations. You may be experiencing something through one of your five senses, but also pay attention to interoceptive sensations such as heat or cold, pain or ease, anxiety or calm, dizziness or stability, strength or shakiness.

3. Take a walk around your house, maintaining contact with your center. Now pay attention to proprioceptive sensations such as balance, coordination, boundaries, or how your body is in motion. You may also notice your heart rate, your breathing, your body's arousal or fatigue, how you might be sensing stress or relaxation in your body.

4. Let yourself feel whatever the prominent sensations are— temperature, pressure, movement, heart rate, breath, where your body is in space, how you sense your balance or imbalance. Just feel what you feel. Stay with any sensations that arise. You might even play with increasing the intensity of the sensation and seeing

how that feels. Follow any emotion that arises; don't push it away. Return again to the pure sensation, and see what it might have to tell you.

5. Grab your notebook and pen and write about the sensations that arose for you, how and where you felt them most, what memory or images may have arisen. Stay with describing what is as much as you can.

6. Later in the day ask yourself: How can knowing, feeling, and naming my sensations help to inform my writing? Spend at least fifteen minutes answering that question for yourself.

3
Postures of Authenticity

I remember an older woman in a workshop I gave many years ago at a poetry festival in Telluride. I had led the group in a centering and body-awareness practice, much like the practice you just did in the previous chapter, and then had them write. Afterward, the woman told me: "At first I noticed that I was all scrunched over my page, my body was curled in on itself, and I thought about how this is always how I sit when I write. Then I remembered our centering practice, and I unfurled myself and felt my length. As I did this, what was remarkable was that I began to know what to write about. Before I had been struggling; now my pen started to move across the page. What a delight!"

This is about much more than posture, much more than the admonition many of us heard from our teachers or parents: "Sit up straight!" This woman "unfurled" her body, and this gave her access to language anew. She tapped into her writer-self, the one who is always available to us if we can find a way to access her. She experienced how centering can help us shift our state of consciousness before we write.

Consider again what your experience was when you practiced centering in your length, width, and depth at the end of the previous chapter. When we center in our length, we work with occupying more of our own vertical space. As we experience being longer, we might also feel our "be-longing" anew. When we feel into our length, we also feel into our sense of dignity. We notice what we feel in this new shape. It is

18

generally surprising to begin to occupy a different kind of space within ourselves and also in relationship to the world.

As we move into an experience of the physical dimension of width, we feel out to the edges of our skin, from head to toes, and then farther out, beyond our bodies. A sense of curiosity always helps this exploration. The dimension of width is the territory of inclusiveness. Width represents our capacity to include others in our attention.

When we move into the physical dimension of depth, we allow ourselves to feel deeply within our bodies—our organs, our hearts and guts and lungs—and also to feel our backs and the field behind us, along with feeling the front of our bodies and the field in front of us. Depth is who we are at the core of ourselves and right beside that are our histories and our longing. We place ourselves firmly in who we are in the present moment and extend with our imaginations to include our past and our desired future.

When we're centered, we are the most authentic, the most trustworthy. Our seeing opens up. We're present to ourselves and the world around us, ready to receive whatever is on offer and able to connect deeply with what is in us as well as around us. When we're centered, we're able to open ourselves to what is given while also sensing the solid ground we reside on. Much like the Telluride woman who couldn't find words from a scrunched-up posture, we can't see out and around ourselves with our heads bowed and our chests collapsed. Just consider walking down the street in a mood of resignation or depression, with a body posture that's collapsed in on itself. What do you see of the world around you? What is possible in your thinking and being? Then consider opening your chest and raising your head to a level position above your shoulders and letting yourself feel the breath run up and down the centerline of your body. Now when you walk, what might you notice?

There's been plenty of research done on the science behind taking certain body postures and the effect this has on our hormonal levels and experience. Even getting into an open pose for only minutes can increase testosterone levels and lower cortisol levels. Because testosterone is the power hormone, and cortisol is the stress hormone, we could say that in open postures our bodies give us different information—most basically, we feel powerful rather than stressed. We can feel ourselves anew in open postures and see what's possible from an unfurled location. And further, in relationship to our writing lives, as we allow ourselves to take more open postures or a more open stance, to feel ourselves as more open and alive, we are more able to say what we need to say. We can write from a place that is authentic.

 *Practice This*
Arriving Home

Felt sense, a phrase coined by American philosopher Eugene Gendlin, is a bodily sense of a situation, person, or event. It's not our thoughts or our words about something, but an internal, deep-down, perhaps unfamiliar, sometimes murky—but always present—knowing. We can access this felt sense when we put our attention into what Gendlin names "the middle of your body," when we listen and feel.[1]

1. Stand, feel your chest rising and falling as you breathe deeply in and out from your abdomen, your hara. Feel your legs holding you. Turn your hips from right to left, generating your movement from your center. Let your arms follow your hip movement. Do this at least a half-dozen times, and then settle.

2. Then say to yourself, "I am arriving home," and pay attention to your body. Ask yourself what arriving home feels like. Just be quiet and listen. Where does home live in you? Luxuriate there.

3. If you need to further experience this sense of moving from center and then settling, repeat the movement in step 1.

4. When you feel complete, take five to ten minutes to write down what you noticed about arriving home and how home lives in you.

 ## Practice This
Power Pose

Here's a chance to experiment with an open posture to see what effect bodily openness might have on your writing as well as your relationship to your writing.

1. Think Wonder Woman. Stand with your feet hip-width apart and place your hands on each of your hips. Stand tall. Look out toward the horizon. Open up your peripheral vision. Feel energy moving down through your legs into the earth. Stand for a minute or two in this posture and see what shifts in your sense of yourself.

2. Now try an expansive posture. Stand again with your legs hip-width apart and open your arms out to each side, parallel to the ground, palms facing upward. Feel the way this opens your entire front body. Ground deeply through your legs. What do you notice in this posture?

3. Which of these practices feels most right to you? Brings you to authenticity? Is it settling into yourself enough to know what it is to arrive home? Is it centering? Is it the power pose?

4. If it is none of these, what posture of your own can you find that allows you to feel what you are made of and what you want to bring forth into language?

5. Choose one and commit to practicing it every day, even several times a day. Take notes on what you learn.

4

Aligning Head, Heart, and Hara: The Column

*T*here are many ways to be a centered human being. Of course, we don't always live from center nor is this even possible—we *are* human! What we can do is to increase our chances of coming from a centered place by practicing in every imaginable situation. It's important to practice when you are not triggered as well as when you are so that you can build your centered "muscles." Consciously bring centering practice into your days by practicing as many times in the day as you can. I don't mean thinking about how good it would be to be centered. Instead, seat yourself in your hara and center in your length, width, depth, and care. Experiment with open postures throughout your day to see what effect this has on yourself and others.

You can also practice centering by consciously aligning the energy centers of head, heart, and hara. You literally bring the three centers into one column. "The column isn't a concept; it's a physical space" is the way my friend Marsha put it when she first experienced this kind of alignment. Much like the power pose, it's a posture, yes, but it is also much more than a posture. When we align these very powerful centers in our being, we give ourselves access to each center as well as to the triad, wholly. When your head, heart, and hara are aligned, you can arrive at a place of both acceptance and conviction within yourself. It's a fearless stance—if by fearless what we mean is the ability to be truly responsive to whatever feelings, sensations, emotions, and knowing arise.

 ## Practice This
Bringing Yourself to the Column

You've worked with a centering practice that allowed you to feel into your body in a manner that may or may not come naturally to you. This practice gives you another means of feeling your body with focus on breath, energy fields, sensation, and alignment of three main energy centers: head, heart, and hara.

1. In a standing position, bring attention first to your breath. Inhale deeply, imagining your breath is spiraling upward from hara to third eye, and then spiraling downward as you exhale back to hara. Give each inhale and exhale at least three counts. As you breathe, let yourself notice whatever sensations arise in you. No judgment, just what is.

2. Next check into the energetic fields that exist all around you: front, back, left, right, above, below. We live in relationship to these energetic fields. In attending to this by asking our bodies how we live in relationship to each of these directions, we come to know where we could expand into more. We ask: Is the field behind me equal to the field in front of me? We set ourselves up to be curious and to feel. Again, just let yourself feel and notice.

3. Then feel the sensation of gravity in your body—let yourself feel the sense of weight and how it grounds you. Let gravity do its work by bringing attention to feeling your own weight and heft on the earth. Let gravity hold you; there's no need to hold yourself up in any manner.

4. Now that you have felt your breath, the energetic fields that surround you, and the force of gravity, ask yourself what you notice. You may already be experiencing yourself differently. Or maybe not. If you are feeling yourself anew, jot down what is different. What do you see, feel, or hear from this place? What are your sensations telling you right now?

5. This is your chance now to both relax into this posture and to shift

something in that posture if you are not feeling aligned in head, heart, and hara. Again, deepen your breath, feel out into the energetic fields that surround you, and let gravity hold you. Now take note of the three centers of head, heart, and hara. Be curious. If you sense that one or more centers is out of alignment—maybe your head is jutting forward or maybe your hara is pulled back—consciously bring yourself into the column. Let your head rest naturally on your shoulders, not leaning left or right, forward or back. Open your chest and place a hand on your heart if that helps you relax and settle. Check in with your hara to sense whether your pelvis is pushed forward or leaning back in any manner. Just notice and adjust.

6. Ask yourself: How is my body lining up with itself anew right now? What difference does this make to me? Take out your notebook and write about life from the column in as much detail as you can.

Center has its own intelligence. From centered presence we know what to say. Doubt tends to ebb away. Our thinking self quiets. Centered gives us access to a larger field. There's no second-guessing here; there's decisiveness. Centered gives us a place to return to within ourselves. Yes, we might still get caught in old patterns or behavior, but through centering, we can move in and out of the caught places more quickly.

As we learn to ask our bodies *how* we live in relationship to the energetic fields around us, we come to know where we might expand into more. If you notice your head tends to want to pull back, you might intentionally exaggerate the placement of your head and see what this brings up for you. Exaggerate the tendency, then let it go and see where your head naturally wants to reside. You can do this with each of these centers, noticing, perhaps, the way your heart begs for protection so you collapse in your chest. Exaggerate the collapse and ask yourself what you need to know from this place of protection. Then open your heart and ask what is revealed now. Asking the question brings us to that state of curiosity, and feeling the sensations that arise as we imagine into each center brings us utterly to the present moment. Learn to live and write from this place of clarity and conviction.

5

Centering in Intention and Care

*W*hat if centering is a posture of fearlessness that makes your life and work better? Centering can help us to be utterly present in the midst of what might otherwise feel dangerous. Danger comes in many shapes—driving down a winding road in the dark, facing a difficult conversation, sitting down at our writing desks with the blank page. When we're centered, we're responsive in the best of ways because we're fully with ourselves. Our peripheral vision opens, and we make ourselves ready for whatever comes.

As you learn more and more about what it means to be centered in your own body and experience, you will likely see that the world looks different from center. There's a clarity and a focus that you have access to that might not have been there before. From a centered state you can begin to see and feel an aliveness and even a sense of purpose that may not have been evident from other states of being. From center you're settled enough that you can begin to see what you want to create or declare.

The act of intending or declaring is a powerful act. We center ourselves by using our breath, dropping our attention, grounding, and sensing how we reside in the physical dimensions of length, width, and depth or how we can align ourselves into the column. But a vital part of the centering practice is to include an intention: What is that larger purpose or commitment I am centering *in*? Where do I want to place my attention and my care?

I once had an experience in the Strozzi Institute dojo while I was speaking with another student, telling her what it is I care about, how I love both language and the ways in which I can move and learn on the aikido mats. After I talked and responded to her questions, she said back to me: "Oh, you want to start a poetry dojo!" I still remember how those words took my breath away and gave me breath at the same time. I also remember when I said the words aloud to the larger group in the dojo, I could feel (and hear!) their collective intake of breath.

This is a way of pointing intent from centered presence. The words *poetry dojo* led me to a physical recognition—that there was this shape I could enter and experience. I could create this space where both language and body were given equal weight. I got there through a centering practice, and then through talking with a good listener about what I care about. Through this process, I was able to express and clarify my care and intention.

What is this relationship between center and intent? When we center, we enter a clearer space from which an intention can take shape. Our minds and judgments quiet. Our intent steadies us. Our words can be powerful tools in defining what is possible, and center helps us get to those words. I remember Marsha telling me about working with her two different intentions, one of being an artist, the other of being an icon maker. She said: "I was astonished at the clarity of the difference. I felt sickened by art. Being an icon maker glows in me." She refined her intention through body and language. She felt both the glow and the sickness and could consciously choose the glow of being an icon maker.

Another story around centering and intending is about an experience I had with center and language, again in the dojo. In the aikido dojo, my experience of learning a *kata* or form with the weapon called a *jo* (a wooden staff about three feet long) had been difficult. I just couldn't remember the thirty-one moves of this kata. But when I practiced centering alongside declaring an intention and feeling into what I care about, I found it possible to finally learn the thirty-one-count kata.

When I said out loud what I was committed to *and* put this beside the body form, I learned the jo kata without any trouble. Making the statement in language, to myself and to others, and sensing into how my body related to my commitment cemented the movements in me. There was suddenly a reason for them that made sense in *all* of myself. It was no longer about rote memorization, but rather about including all of myself in the learning—especially my care and, of course, my body.

Here is the heart of much of somatic work: that to learn and indeed to transform, we have to contact or connect with what we care about and feel this emotional engagement as we center ourselves in the lives we're living and create the life we desire. Indeed, the word *soma* means the living body in its wholeness, and of course this wholeness includes noticing our physical structure and movement, our breath, our attention, a sense of gravity—alongside what our vision is and how we want to manifest that vision.

 *Practice This*

Accessing the Care of Your Heart

As we learn to increase our clarity and focus through the practice of centering, we also begin to see the growing relationship between centered presence and intent. Centering can help us find the words to name what is possible. We find out what we deeply care about when we can allow and listen to the stillness.

1. Stand facing an open space—it may be a field, the sky, a blank wall. Stand squarely with your feet hip-distance apart. Let yourself settle by taking a few deep breaths or closing your eyes or deepening your stance by sensing energy moving down through your legs and into the earth.

2. Place your right hand over your heart and your left hand over your right. Take a few seconds to feel the support you are providing yourself right now. Feel into the field all around you—right, left, front, back. Feel yourself at the center of this field you're making. Then notice that you are in relationship to its pulse and life as much as you are to your own pulse and life.

3. Look into that open space. Let your hands come down by your sides, palms facing forward. Ask yourself one or more of these questions:
   - What's at the edge of this field that is calling to me?
   - What do I want to create or make happen in my life?
   - What do I deeply care about?
   - Where and how do I feel that care in my body?

4. Let the words arise from the stillness within you. Allow them to surface. Listen. Be curious. Something may come quickly—or perhaps it may take some time or multiple repetitions of this practice.

5. As the words arise, feel free to speak them aloud, or write them down, or both.

6. If you're having trouble, place your hands on your heart again and ask yourself: What matters most to me?

7. Let the words come—anything that spills forth—until you feel complete. Speak the words aloud, or write them, or both. If you like, take five minutes to write everything that surfaced in answer to these questions.

8. Afterward—whatever your experience has been—ask yourself the following questions:
   - What most stands out about what I just experienced?
   - What do I most care about?
   - Where does that care reside in my body? How does that care feel?
   - What do I want to create in my life now?
   - What can I intend or commit to in relationship to this care I've discovered? Commit to paper what you've discovered:
     I care about . . .
     I intend to . . .
     I commit to . . .

9. This care is part of what you can now center in, with, and through. Bring this commitment into your centering practice—what you center in your physical being, your care, your commitment. Bring the care and the commitment right into your writing life.

6

Following Center's Intelligence into Your Work

*A*s we are finding, center is a connected place from which we are both deeply who we are—without agenda or desire—and deeply connected to other humans, to the natural world, and to our care. What better place than this is there to let words form in us—and fall onto the page? We've been exploring how being in a centered state can lead us into a clearer, more appropriate, fearless means of expressing ourselves. When we're centered, we're more able to listen. Center itself gives us access to a deeper, wider, more inclusive listening. When we're centered, our perceptions can open up to encompass the *other* in a new way. Curiously, center allows us to be less self-centered.

My painter friend Marsha often speaks of how center can bring her to the true subject of the painting, that she finds herself "in the midst of paint" and from here she brings her aliveness to the centered state. She says from this space she is not asking her paintings to be commodities, but rather to be "icons of centered chi." The centered state only leads her into curiosity and to the dance of self and work.

In a centered state we are more deeply relaxed, and within that is an opportunity to contact our strength. Center has affected my writing in so many ways, but I also note a big difference in how I read my work in public. I literally feel the words as they move through my body. It's as if language fully occupies me, from the inside out, so that language is then born out of the body. It's as if language and body are really one. There's an intense aliveness in this place—electric, pulsing, reverberating.

Center can bring us to a new confidence in the work itself. Work that is derived from center has a different trustworthiness to it. Focusing on the breath and on posture allows for a different kind of discernment as we create. We let breath and posture lead rather than any kind of perceived critical voice from within or without. As we become more settled and less fearful, our work becomes more alive, too. Once centered we can remind ourselves of a sense of dignity in our own experience, and then walk through the door to that experience on the page. *All I can be is who I am,* center says.

Centered writing can certainly arise when we get better and better at being centered and also at being able to point our intent toward the work at hand. What if you let center write your next piece? The state of being out of which language arrives can be one of centered presence—a state that is alert, attentive, focused, clear, without agenda, open, connected, and alive to what is.

 *Practice This*
Two-Step

Yes, centering brings you to your most alert, alive, and confident self. As you practice centering you begin to build a body that can return, again and again, to that open and connected place. But taking centering fully into your life requires you to move with your center, to change direction and still be centered, to get jolted off course and be able to return to your center. The following practice helps you bring center into action.

1. Begin by centering, of course! At this point you have several possibilities available to you for coming to center. Choose one of your favorites. It might be centering in length, width, and depth.

It might be that you take several deep breaths; notice the fields above, below, in front of, and behind you; and drop your attention to your hara and feel the stillness. It might be that you love the column, and you spend some time aligning head, heart, and hara into that vertical column. You might want to focus on sensations or on breath or on feeling inside yourself and then outside yourself. Whatever it is that intrigues you about your centering practice, go there.

2. Let yourself feel sufficiently resourced by center—settled in yourself, present to yourself and your surroundings, connected and open to what wants to come into form. Now let's learn a new move.

3. The two-step is a great way to build centering in action into your body-self. Sometimes I two-step to feel myself come into align-ment with all of myself and, from there, to fill myself with intention (or even with joy).

4. Put your left foot in front of your right at a comfortable distance, one that allows you to feel solidly placed on the earth. Bend your knees slightly as you face forward. Settle by taking a few breaths from hara.

5. Next, step forward with your right foot, beyond where your left foot is. Pivot on the ball of your right foot and turn your body as you bring your left foot completely behind you. You're now facing the opposite direction from where you began. Now your right foot is in front (as illustrated on p. 32). Step-turn again—left foot comes forward, pivot on it, turn and bring your right foot behind. Keep doing this move until you don't have to think about it.

Here are some pointers for refinement as you practice, over and over, each day:
- Move from hara or center.
- Don't look at your feet—look up and out, beyond yourself.
- Breathe.
- Let your arms flow with your body as you turn.
- Smile.

A. *This is the beginning of the two-step move. After starting with the left leg in front of the right, you then step forward with the right foot, shown here.*

B. *This shows the pivot move with the right foot as the body begins to turn and the left foot moves behind you.*

C. *This shows the final position in the two-step move, with the right foot in front and the left behind, with the body facing in a new direction.*

 ## *Practice This*
Centering and Two-Stepping around an Idea

At this point you may have become discombobulated by learning a new move. That's OK. Lots is always available to us to shake us from our centers! But what I want you to do now is to return to your center. Once you have returned, you will have the opportunity to experiment with the two-step and a color, letting images and memories arise as you move.

1. Use your breath, drop your attention, feel the fields all around you, smile, and know that you just learned a new two-stepping move that could serve you in many ways. We're going to try one way.

2. Let yourself choose a color. Just let the color arise. Don't think about it. What color immediately emerged? Write it down on a small piece of paper (something that you can readily step around).

3. Place the piece of paper on the floor in front of you. Look at your color. Let it enter you. Say its name over and over and just let any images or thoughts arise as you do so.

4. Now ready yourself to two-step around your color. You can do this by facing the piece of paper on the floor and placing your left foot in front of your right. (By now you have practiced the two-step move enough that I don't have to talk you through it. But if you are not yet comfortable with the move, return to practicing it, as described above.)

5. Now step-turn around your color. As you do so, let your color enter into you, under your skin, into your cells. Keep moving: step-turn, step-turn. If it's possible to do so without losing your balance, you might try closing your eyes and letting the color into the darkness behind your eyes—make the darkness be your color. You can speed up or slow down in whatever way you please, just be sure to be dancing with your color.

6. When you feel you've danced your way into your color, stop and let yourself settle. Keep holding your color close to your heart and in the soles of your feet.

7. Now sit down and write about your color. What images arose as you two-stepped with your color? Follow them. What memories are speaking to you now? What do you have to say about your color that you never realized before? Just keep writing and writing until your color gets to fully tell you who it is.

7

What's Revealed through Practice

*W*e know that to get better at anything at all requires practice: just ask any athlete, musician, artist, writer, or public speaker how they got where they are. You've probably heard the quote, sometimes attributed to professional golfer Arnold Palmer: "It's a funny thing, the more I practice, the luckier I get." The more we place our bodies "on the line," the more responsive we become in the moment. Remember we can always place ourselves in the dojo. We can always cross the threshold, try on a new way of being.

In the aikido dojo we practice the same techniques over and over again. I am always amazed at how different the same technique can feel with a different partner, on a different day, in another mood. What we learn through our bodies and through recurrent practice makes change possible. Consistency helps the practice take root in us.

Consider for a moment your writing life, whatever that means to you right now. Maybe you write every day in a journal to hone your attention to the written word. You consciously choose to write in your journal as a practice that helps you to embody your writing life. Such a practice doesn't just make you able to write in your journal, it will likely help you considerably when you turn your attention to writing a poem or a novel or a blog post. This makes the practice generative—

wherever you turn, under whatever context, you are becoming a writer.

Two qualities are essential for practice to truly take root in you and effect change. One is that when you practice you attend to how you show up in the practice. You let yourself be aware of *how* you practice. For example, when you practice the two-step move that you learned in the last chapter, it's important to ask yourself *how you are* in the movement, in the practice. As you bring more and more awareness to yourself as you practice, you can begin to expand your ability to see, feel, and know how to build on your presence in that practice.

The other quality to bring to your practice is a sense of why you're doing the practice, what it is you want to grow into or to change. To keep to the two-step move, maybe you're practicing the two-step so that you can get better at shifting from your day job to your writing desk with a clear intent for that day's writing. You two-step with the intention of taking your centered, alive presence from your job to your writing. This matters to you, of course. So you two-step with curiosity, asking how you're showing up. What's your mood? What do you notice about how you sense your body in space? Are you clumsy or graceful (no judgment, just what is)? What can you adjust in breath, posture, or movement to feel more centered and grounded as you two-step?

Change happens when we're willing to "take it to the mats," which is to step into all the arenas of our lives with body, heart, and soul open and connected, moving with spirit and intention. We have to practice our way into a fuller way of being. Often our arena of practice is revealed to us through paying attention to where our rough spots reside. It could also be that a friend or a teacher points something out to us that opens us to that arena of practice. One time an aikido sensei pointed out to me a longtime pattern I had of turning away with my body as I executed a technique. I knew that turning away made me unable to succeed in redirecting the energy of my partner on the aikido mats. But I also knew that to live every part of my life fully—personal relationships as well as writing life—I had to turn toward. I remember taking this practice around the world with me as I traveled—literally noticing as I was in conversation with someone I'd just met that I wasn't fully facing him or her. In the moment of that noticing, I would shift my hips toward the other—center to center—resulting in a fuller, richer conversation. I found that courage lives in this gesture of turning toward and that fear dissipates.

At another time, I'd taken up swimming and decided to bring intention to it and make it into a generative practice, one that could ripple out into my life outside the pool. I realized pretty quickly that I was more interested in the metaphor of swimming than in becoming a better swimmer. I remember swimming slowly and feeling myself stroke by stroke in the water, getting nowhere in particular, but realizing I was building a body that's stronger and happier because of it. I felt, too, a deepening quality of immersion as I swam—and I recall realizing that what I really wanted was *a body of work I could swim in*. I laughed, backstroking down the lane. It was something about the naturalness, the full immersion, the splash that I loved. At the time Marsha responded in a letter to me: "I feel about tai chi the way you wrote about swimming, never thinking 'this swim is so damn good it should be published.'" What I learned in this practice remains invaluable to me now: it's the day-to-day slow immersion that matters; it's feeling myself and the world stroke by stroke that matters. Sometimes what's important is to keep feeling the practice until it reveals to you what needs to be seen.

Bringing practice into all you do and all you are helps you to arrive at the next turning. When we bring practice deeply into the terrain of our lives, we make the changes that are necessary to the lives we want to create. Through repetition, attention, movement, and emotional engagement, we come to embody our learning and make changes that are lasting. What matters most to each of us can then find its powerful and rightful place in our lives and in the world.

Practice This
Refining Practice

Choosing a practice you love enough to stay with over time, finding the relevance in that particular practice to what you are developing in yourself and in your writing, being curious about what you are learning, and always asking yourself how you are showing up in the practice are all essential qualities of building practices into your writing life that expand and brighten who you are as a writer.

1. Consider what practices you are currently engaged in, either related to your life or to your writing. These could be practices that you have not yet seen as being a practice, necessarily. For example, maybe you have a sitting practice or a yoga practice or you walk, bike, or run regularly. Maybe you've taken on one of the practices in this book. What is the practice of your choice right here, right now, that you most want to explore?

2. What brought you to this practice in the first place? Write about your practice now.

3. Consider what you've noticed about yourself to this point when engaging in the practices presented in this book. When you center, what have you seen or felt? Maybe you have a tendency to turn away from direct experience as I did, and you know this affects your abilities as a writer and communicator, and you'd like that to change. Or maybe you've noticed a forward lean in yourself that makes you feel that you're about to fall over or it makes you feel that you rush through life and you don't want to do that anymore. You want to savor experience, feel it more than you already do.

4. From what you've noticed in these practices, is there something that you'd like to change or to develop even more in yourself?

5. I'd like you to think about your current practice a bit differently now. First ask yourself this: How could this practice generate a new quality in me, one that I've wanted for a long time but can't seem to achieve? How does this quality relate to my writing?

6. Why is it important to me that I learn to embody this quality? How will embodying this quality affect my writing?

7. Now that you know what your practice has been or you've chosen one to focus on, enter into your practice anew. Before you do the practice, tell yourself why you are practicing and why it matters to you that you embody this new quality. As you practice remember what and why you're practicing.

8. As you practice, pay attention to who you are in the practice. Are you excited, annoyed, attentive, fuzzy, focused? Let yourself widen your awareness to include both what's going on inside yourself and what's going on in your surroundings.

9. Feel into how committed you are to this practice and to your growth as a writer. Let yourself be filled with your intention for this deepening that you are asking for. Keep practicing.

10. Write down in your journal what your practice is, how many times each week you will engage in this practice, and how you will record what you notice as you practice.

Part Two

Opening the Body to Language

- ▶ Find ways to enter your solitude and begin to hear the sound of your own voice; you'll discover spaciousness.

- ▶ Learn how discomfort can serve as a doorway, and cross the threshold to the emergence of your writing, bringing presence to whatever arises.

- ▶ Explore the space of not knowing.

- ▶ See how crucial it is to make your writing rich with the particular.

- ▶ Experience deep listening and the ways in which silence can open you to your intuition.

- ▶ Begin to come into your own through a deeper understanding of how you live in your body and in language.

- ▶ Start writing from the new shape you are becoming.

- ▶ Identify what you need to be supported in your writing life and begin to bring that in energetically.

8

Your Dojo of Solitude

*M*any years of practice in an aikido dojo taught me the significance and value of showing up at a particular time and place, no matter my mood or inclination, and engaging intimately with other bodies on the mats. We would stretch and prepare our bodies and psyches to meet the other. Then we would do so, over and over, as we practiced one technique after another for the duration of the class. Day after day, I entered the dojo in one state of mind and body and left renewed, refreshed, even shining. There's power in defining a space and stepping into it wholeheartedly.

Your writing space can be a dojo, too. But it is a space you enter alone, which is why I'm naming it your "dojo of solitude." Standing in your solitude, you'll find the time and space to write and to learn what it means to face yourself. You'll find this place of no distractions where you can hear the sound of your own voice. As the founder of aikido noted many times: the mats are a place of polishing our rough spots, polishing our spirits. We can also polish ourselves as writers in our writing dojo.

What you're doing is to define a space, and then to make things happen there. Simple enough, right? It makes a difference to declare your writing space as dojo and to claim your solitude. The literal space in which you do this is crucial. Luckily, there are many options available to make your own dojo of solitude.

Writing spaces that allow for solitude are as different as we all are as writers. If there's an extra room in your house that you can claim as your own and make into your writing dojo, do that. Maybe it's just a corner of a room where you can put a desk and make it yours alone. I once made a hallway leading to my bedroom into my study—it provided the quiet and aloneness I needed. But maybe you are someone who finds solitude among a multitude of others. I remember my friend Natalie always saying that she had to leave the house and go to a café to write— the din sent her into herself, into her space of solitude, which allowed writing to happen. Another writer I know didn't have private space in his house in which to write, so he wrote at the kitchen table when no one else was around. He surrounded himself with books and papers related to the writing he was engaged in at the time and defined his space right there among the spices and pans. Libraries are great places to find a quiet corner. Or maybe you like writing in a park or restaurant or even a bar. The time of day can also help you create your dojo—stay up late or get up early to find your solitude. If you have a job, stay late at your desk after work, but do your own writing—might even lead to a raise, who knows? The point is to find what works for you, to give yourself the gift of solitude in whatever flavor suits you.

A dojo is a place of awakening. When we enter our writing space as a dojo, we know we might have rough days when we are challenged to get the words out or to fully embrace our identities as writers. Sometimes we find it difficult to fully meet the other in the shape of our characters, our lives, the fence post we're trying to describe. By naming a space as your dojo, you're reminding yourself of the importance of carving out a space and time in which to get your work done. This allows you to awaken to what that work is and to value that work enough that you make a nest for it. You feed it; you tend to it until it shines.

Showing up is of course the first step. As you cross the threshold into your writing space, you might even adopt a bow as a way of entering. Once in, you can be assured that you will encounter yourself and your raw material anew. No doubt you'll learn and discover something in the process. And, yes, you will awaken as your material begins to awaken within you.

Practice This

Finding Your Dojo of Solitude

In this practice you'll come to know what difference it makes to create your own sacred space for your writing. Your writing dojo becomes a container for your solitude and the blossoming of your writing life. But everyone is fed differently, and it is up to each of us to find the qualities and nuances of our own dojo.

1. Find a space outdoors that gives you pleasure and buoyancy, a place that feeds you in some manner. Stand facing as much openness as the space provides.

2. Take four deep breaths, letting in the openness. Feel your feet on the ground and sense the energy running down your legs and into the earth. If you notice your knees locking, gently bend and unbend your knees, letting in more fluidity.

3. Close your eyes and settle. Place your right hand over your heart and your left hand over your right and settle some more.

4. Ask yourself: Where's my dojo? As you ask the question, just notice and allow whatever happens. Gently ask the question again if nothing much arises. You might find that words come—if so, speak aloud where your dojo is. Describe it. Or you might find that an image is forming. If that happens, keep asking until what you see comes more and more into focus. If you notice that any part of you tightens, take a moment to breathe into the constricted place before you ask again.

5. Then swivel your hips from side to side as if you're doing the twist (dating myself here!). Move your shoulders up, down, and around to loosen any tightness there. Then return to holding both hands at your heart and asking: What is my dojo? Again, let words or images arise. Keep loose, walk around if that helps you, remembering to settle yourself again when you stop moving.

6. What have you seen, felt, or learned about where or what your dojo is? Speak aloud what you now know about your dojo.

Once you locate your dojo, you can enter it again and again, taking with you that shift in consciousness as you cross the threshold. You can do this anywhere, actually. Once you cross the threshold into your dojo, you may realize that although it's a dojo of solitude, you are actually not alone. As you settle and listen, you may notice that characters or other humans may emerge and take up space beside and within you. Ideas that you've only begun to have while engaged in your busy life can now take root. As you deepen in your solitude, you can empty yourself of striving, pushing, or doing and hear the words that want to fill the page. You might remember scenes from your life or create ones anew. And your body is part of this process because your body is the vessel through which words are formed and take shape on the page. In your dojo of solitude, you can quiet yourself enough to let your own thoughts rise, form themselves into language, find themselves written down on a page.

To write anything at all, we have to cultivate and honor our ability to have our own thoughts, to get those thoughts down, to stand up and move about and consider how what arises from deep within us has anything at all to do with anyone else. It does. Even in the dojo of solitude we are always acting in relationship—to all that is and all that has been in our lives. Solitude opens the door. The more we can allow ourselves to experience and deepen in our solitude, the more we can give shape to the invisible. What lives deep within us can rise up out of us and emerge as words on a page.

Maybe solitude is unnerving to you or possibly frightening. But we must go deeply into the dark and the light. Wherever it is that we go in the dojo of solitude—sometimes to the dark, other times to the light— we can build our capacity to stay with ourselves. To not only have our own thoughts but to communicate them, live beside them, wrestle with them, get them down in our own language.

In your dojo of solitude, you can uncover what you don't yet know and move forward, even at those times when you don't have a clue where you're headed. In the dojo of solitude, you can awaken to the mystery. You can accept yourself as you are, be with what is. You can be with other creatures, humans, thought-forms, time zones. It is an all-expansive place, this dojo of solitude. You enter it not knowing. You surface from it shining.

Practice This
Getting to Know Your Dojo:
Asking Slowly, Creating Space

This practice is a beginning, a way in, a means of creating space, what-ever that means to you, and entering it. A way into language. We define the space, and then we make things happen there. Entering your dojo of solitude has a quality of ritual to it. Bowing as you enter the space makes it clear to yourself that you are changing worlds.

1. Enter your dojo. As you cross the threshold of that physical space, take a bow. If there's a door into your dojo, close it behind you.

2. Set a timer to go off in five minutes.

3. Sit comfortably, legs crossed if on a cushion, or feet simply placed on the ground if in a chair. Let your back be as straight as you can, close your eyes, and begin to breathe deeply. Let your inhale originate from hara, then travel up to the crown of your head, then your exhale travel back down to hara. Give your inhale and exhale four counts each. Attempt to focus only on your breath, counting in four, then out four. If you feel any tension in your body, gently place a hand there as you continue to breathe in and out.

4. If your mind wanders, ruminates, or gets activated in any way, as it very well might, bring your attention to this line from a poem: "I ask these questions slowly / because they have no answer." Say this line to yourself, then return to your breath. When your timer goes off, move slowly to a pen and paper. Ask: If I were to define a space for my writing dojo, what would it look like? Remember back to the first practice in this chapter when you went outdoors and began to feel into where and what your dojo is. Ask yourself now: What do I want to make happen there?

5. Write for five minutes without stopping. Find your way into your own dojo and your own words.

 *Practice This*

Developing a Ritual for Your Dojo of Solitude

As I said earlier, in the aikido dojo I sometimes showed up in a state of disarray. Although it wasn't always easy, through engaging with the practices in the dojo, I would find my way back to a more settled, clear state. I would bow and then go to the dressing room and change into a different outfit, the *gi*. Both of these acts helped me to see and feel that the space is a sacred one. As you enter into your own dojo alone, you can also prepare yourself.

1. Consider your outfit. What would make you feel especially dapper as you enter into your writing dojo? Wear that! If *dapper* isn't your word or preferred way of being, find another and wear that.

2. As you approach the threshold of your dojo in your special clothing, pause before entering the space. Bow if that feels good to you. If it's not a bow, try another movement before entering (jumping, turning, smiling, holding a hand to your heart—anything that feels right to you and that helps you contact another state of being). Now you can step into your dojo of solitude.

3. Then have a practice that brings you more fully into the space. You have several that have been introduced thus far in this book—choose a centering practice that you like the most. Be sure to quiet yourself with several deep breaths, feel your ground and feel the space all around you. Only when you are ready, approach the page.

4. When you complete your writing session, you may find it helpful to have a way back into the world outside your dojo. The two-step you learned earlier could serve you well here. Complete your writing, put it all away, stand in the center of your space, settle yourself, and two-step. This move helps with centering in transition, so let it serve you in this way. If you feel wobbly, stop and settle some more, then resume the two-step. Let yourself be as fluid as you can. Enjoy the move. As you're two-stepping, you might ask: What am I moving into next? And let the two-step serve to get you there.

5. When you leave your dojo of solitude, you can even bow out. As you cross back over the threshold, turn and face your space and take a deep bow of gratitude and appreciation for the writing you faced today and for what you accomplished.

9

Creating Space and Spaciousness

*I*deally, the dojo you create holds rigor and compassion in equal measure. You cross over that threshold, enter your writing dojo, and begin. But what does beginning look like? And who is the *you* who begins? In the writing dojo, we're aiming for the accuracy and precision of right thought and right words, of finding the language that resonates with our own heart and soul. It's rigor for what is true, what is deeply so, what best reflects our thinking and being. Compassion is a good companion to have beside rigor. We must learn to bear our own difficulties as we stride deeper and deeper into that dojo.

By rigor I don't mean being even harder on yourself than you already are. Save your critical eye for much later on in the writing process, when you see what you've gotten down on the page and you can begin to re-vision it, make it stronger. For now, be rigorous with your intentions for your work. Be rigorous about showing up as much as you possibly can and fully engaging with the page and with yourself. And be compassionate with all the ways that you may fail. Be compassionate with your tender selves that you'll be exposing as you write.

One of the qualities you can choose to bring into your dojo is spaciousness. Rather than rushing from one topic to the next or finishing one project then moving quickly into another or finding yourself in a corner because your critical voices are raging—learn how to create intentional spaciousness. This isn't a squishy place, but rather a place filled with air, light, and breath.

When we sit down at our desks, there are often plenty of voices that start up, that pull our attention, that poke and prod at our idea for what's next on the page. This can lead to a writing session that comes from a constricted place rather than a place of spaciousness. What are your particular voices that ask to be heard as you sit down to write? Is it the "not-enough" voice? Or the "it's already been done" voice? Or the "I'm not really a writer" voice? Or maybe the "if I tell the truth about such-and-such or so-and-so, I will hurt somebody." Or "I feel things strongly, but when I write, nothing comes out as strongly as I feel."

All these voices can cause us to constrict. We have to face each one—not ignore them nor push them aside. They are persistent, and they will just keep talking to us in the background. Clearly, they're asking for attention, so give them attention. Rather than constricting around whatever your particular voice is, turn toward it, be in relationship to it.

 Practice This
Bringing Space to the Constricted Places

You've created your writing dojo, and now you will begin to bring intention into how you fill that dojo with new writing. As you notice the ways in which you tighten around a writing subject or around the act of writing itself, you can then make another choice: you can bring spaciousness into your consciousness and see the ways this alters your work.

1. Walk into your writing dojo. Enter the space slowly. Be attentive as you approach your writing desk. Take your seat or your standing position.

2. Ask yourself what you feel, what you notice. Are you cramped up in your writing seat? Is your head bowed? Are you restless? Do you feel the breath flowing through you, or is it getting stopped somewhere in your body?

3. Now intentionally bring space to your constriction by asking your-
   self these questions:
   - What is a question or belief that causes you to constrict when
     you write? Write it down in your notebook.
   - Speak this question or belief aloud and really let yourself feel
     the impact of your words. Speak again and feel even more.
     Notice what happens in your breath, your gut, your heart, your
     emotions, your posture, as you speak and feel the impact of
     your words on your psyche and body.
   - Exaggerate this shape that your belief or question has created in
     you and feel it some more, really get to know it.
   - Now, whatever is happening, bring breath to it. Stand up if that
     helps, and let the breath come and go from your hara. Walk
     around the room. Feel your ground. Feel your length, width,
     and depth. Consider what really matters to you. Let that into
     your entire being.
   - What are you noticing? What idea has begun to form itself that
     was not there before? What else might you be feeling besides
     the anxiety and constriction you were feeling before? Jot down
     all that you notice in your body-self now.
   - What has shifted in you and what difference does that make to
     your writer-self?

Constricted shapes make us small. Our hearts tighten, chests collapse; we tend to feel less. Often we become ungrounded and literally
cannot feel our feet on the ground; our breath is shallow, maybe we
feel restless. Whatever your constricted shape is, it is certainly a protected one, and you certainly needed it at some point in your life. The
problem comes when you try to create from this constriction. Or even
to live from here. Nothing much is possible other than anxiety from
such a state.

Novelist Anne Lamott says that our goal as writers is to help others
have a sense of wonder: we have to help them see things anew. She adds

that this makes everything feel spacious.[1] French philosopher Gaston Bachelard in *The Poetics of Space* writes about how immensity lives within us and that when we become motionless, we are elsewhere; we can dream ourselves into the immensity of the world then.[2] Spaciousness lives in these places of awe, wonder, and immensity. When we are able to turn our attention toward the immensity of what surrounds us and embrace the depth of the worlds within us, we're in spacious territory.

How do we feel spaciousness in our bodies, though? Often, we can experience spaciousness as the absence of constriction. But first we have to identify the constriction. I recall a client who was frustrated at not getting to the truth, her truth, in her work. This made her feel lethargic, and the lethargy caused her not to get her writing done. When I asked her to identify any sensation in her body that went along with these feelings, she immediately identified "the blob," which she said was a sensation in the vicinity of her heart that felt "viscous, oily, dark, warm." She knew right away that this blob was what was getting in her way of speaking her truth, and that without the blob, she would experience the space in which to ask questions, be curious, explore. Once she identified a physical location and was able to describe the sensations she was experiencing, she was able to work directly with opening the constriction and experiencing spaciousness. Over time this had profound effects on her writing. Once she was able to see the constriction for what it was and to explore how it had protected her, she could open herself to other possibilities. This led to much more truthful work.

Practice This
Identifying the Constriction, Feeling Spaciousness

Making clear the actual physical sensation of what is constricted in us helps us to allow some space to enter into our bodies. Just as my client identified her constriction as "the blob" and was then able to work directly with the sensation and her beliefs associated with it, you can identify sensations and beliefs associated with your constriction. Once identified, the constriction can then begin to soften and open.

1. Consider a recent experience or situation in which you felt defensive, something that made you cringe, or turn away, or shut down in some fashion. Maybe this will be hard for you to access. If so, walk around your writing dojo and let yourself daydream as you walk. What has happened lately that has made you feel pressure from outside yourself?

2. If it's not a recent experience, then it might be a writing topic. Have you been attempting to write about something difficult? Or is there a painful memory that you feel you must face in your writing but cannot? If so, what is that memory?

3. Choose which of the above you want to work with—either the recent experience or situation that made you feel defensive or the writing topic that you're finding challenging.

4. Begin by bringing that experience or challenge into the present moment. Surround yourself either with the voice of that pressure you felt, or let yourself remember the situation or the painful memory. Let it into your whole being.

5. As you re-encounter the difficulty, notice what is happening inside yourself. What is the primary sensation you notice? Remember the blob and ask yourself what your sensation looks like. What is its color? Texture? Temperature? What does it make you feel or believe? Let yourself feel this constriction in your body and in your psyche. Take your notebook out and describe it as richly as you can.

6. Now begin to move around. Loosen. Circle your hips around, clockwise and counterclockwise. Then shake them from side to side. Let the tension caused by the constriction fall away from you. If it helps, you can also shake each leg out. Move your shoulders up to your ears and down again to release any residual tension held there. Take a deep breath and release an exhale in a big sigh. Do this a few times.

7. Now stand and stretch your arms back in an open-chested posture. Tip your head back so that your neck is open. Breathe into these spaces in your chest and in your neck. Do this move several times, being careful to move slowly and not strain your neck. Now settle by standing still and looking out a window at the horizon.

8. Write your reflections in answer to the following questions.
   - What do you notice within yourself?
   - What do you notice in relationship to the constriction you felt
     earlier?
   - What has spaciousness allowed for you?
   - How else might you feel spaciousness as you go about your day?

Often simply asking the question *Can I bring spaciousness even to this moment?* shifts our consciousness enough that the space begins to open up, even just a little. Maybe you'll begin to get hints about what it would be like to write from a wider field. You'll see what it means for you to become aware of the present moment and engage with that rather than be afraid or turn away. When an idea, question, or new thought rises seemingly out of nowhere, give it space and let yourself take the time needed to turn toward the question or idea so that what it wants from you can be revealed. Maybe you can then dance with where you are and write from this sense of dancing.

We all sometimes set ourselves a schedule for writing. We sit down at our desks and feel we must produce. This often gets in the way of our finding what we really want to say. Bringing in spaciousness (and some days, huge amounts of forgiveness) might mean that we aren't doing much of anything. But it's a better choice to find spaciousness and then write, rather than to force ourselves to write because it's scheduled.

A client told me she had an awful writing day of no writing because she put just this kind of time pressure on herself. The schedule had been made, she sat down to engage, and all she could feel was that she couldn't do it, that maybe she's not really a writer, that clearly she wasn't if she couldn't get this book done at last. She suffered in this place; she was tired and hadn't slept much the night before. She was insisting to herself that she write—and likely believed that if she couldn't write it was because she's not a writer anyway. This was her place of constriction. This was her opportunity to notice that first of all and then to create a shift in herself. What if, instead, she gave herself spaciousness? What could that have looked like? What might it look like if you give yourself that spaciousness?

Practice This
Finding and Releasing Constriction around
Your Creative Life

As you've seen in this chapter, constriction can be explored through sensation and also through your strongly held beliefs about yourself and your writing life. The following practice asks you to consider first a constricted belief, then to explore how that belief lives in your body, ultimately bringing in more spaciousness, and thus, more choice.

1. Pick an area of your own creative life that feels constricted.
2. First feel fully into that constriction. Where do you feel it most? What's it look like, feel like, taste like, smell like? What color is it? What's its texture?
3. Now given that you've been practicing feeling your sensations and defining your very own constriction, ask yourself what movement you could make to help you loosen that constriction. Do that.
4. Now approach this constriction by free-writing about it for at least ten minutes. Name the constriction. Describe it in as much detail as you can muster.
5. Then bring some intentional spaciousness to this constriction. Find where the constriction feels most alive in your body, and then consciously bring breath to that place. Stretch that area of your body—literally giving it more space.
6. Write about what you notice.
7. Now, settle more into your ground, into yourself. Increase your awareness of your breath and the space around you and in you that you are now occupying, the space you are bringing to that constricted place in you.
8. What does feeling into that space make possible for you? For your writing life? For your writing?

Whenever you identify a sensation that feels constricting or notice yourself in a body shape that is collapsed or constricted, remember and practice any of what you have experienced throughout this chapter:

- Bring awareness to the sensation you are having.
- Describe it in as much detail as you can.
- Ask what the constriction makes you think or believe.
- Take several deep breaths.
- Move in whatever manner suits you to loosen the constriction.
- Dance with yourself and the constriction.
- Ask yourself what you think or believe now.
- Reapproach the writing at hand from this new place.

10

The Writing Body's Emergence

*W*hat opens you to language? I've sometimes heard writers say that they only write when something is really bothering them, when they feel particularly challenged in a relationship, or when the world is weighing heavily on their psyches. Adversity can open us to listening and calls on a deeper part of ourselves that insists on being heard. Discomfort can serve as a doorway. What challenges us asks us to show up. Courage that might be dormant in our everyday, more comfortable lives surfaces anew.

Writing can help us make sense of our inner lives. Writing can feel like an urgent requirement. Sometimes the whirl of emotions inside us needs a place to land. Writing can help us find refuge and heart in what otherwise feels like a teeming morass. As we dive under the surface, we find what wants to breathe, to be given life. Our writing gives life to what otherwise goes unseen or remains silent. As we write, we discover how language wants to shape itself into our own particular meaning. Adversity can open us to the writing body.

This sense of being pushed out of one's comfort zone, of creating order, of living on the edge and making sense out of that—all this brings us to the page. We have to pay attention to what opens us to language so that we recognize when we are in that rich territory. Much of our writing comes from digging into the darker corners, encountering what's hidden. When we keep digging we sometimes find jewels: a sudden understanding or crystallization of thought where before there had only been muddiness; an image rising that speaks to something we had not seen before and that helps us to see anew. Or the writing itself might lead us through another doorway into a room we have never seen before that we get to touch and feel and know as a child might. We dig in, we ask, and sometimes we just wait.

The poet William Stafford spoke of writing as "the free dive into the experience of now."[1] He advocated for allowing emergence of one's own language and for embracing an attitude of discovery. He wanted us to allow things to come through the door. This attitude implies that we are in a state of readiness, and we need a way to recognize when something does come through the door. This requires a certain presence and awareness. Sometimes the room is empty and we have to wait, to allow emergence. And some days we'll find the words piled up on the other side of the door!

We need a varied set of practices and ways into presence, allowing, and seeing in order to capture our own language on the page. What might this look like? One day it might look like a sitting practice followed by a movement practice followed by a sit-down at the desk and a waiting period, a stillness, until something does, indeed, come through the door. Writing that down. Seeing where that leads. Following a thread. Listening, watching, waiting, and engaging. Letting the words flow out of you in the order they want to. Not controlling a thing.

Another day may be challenging in another sort of way. Maybe you got some bad news. Maybe you woke feeling dispirited and dark but have no clue why. Maybe your dreams were particularly intense and they draped themselves over you this particular morning, a clinging heavy coat. How do you find language when what you really want to do is hide out?

You find a way to surface what's hidden deep within you and craft language from there. This might mean you go for a walk and open yourself to the land surrounding you, take it in, remember that you are part of the world alongside the horny toad, the mountains or sea, the plains or forest, the dirt beneath your feet. You are part of the human and not-human community. Feel that. Find a way to connect to what is larger than you as well as what's within you. Or get really curious about your desire to hide out. What does this particular hiddenness feel like?

It is crucial to find your own way through, to deeply consider what opens you to language, to your own distinct and powerful way of putting words on a page or out into the air we all breathe.

 ## Practice This
What's Knocking at My Door?

As you find more and more ways to increase your presence and awareness, you will also find new ways to connect to the words that want to come through you. The deepening quiet and solitude available to you will help you increase your listening presence and move you into new writing.

1. Set a timer for at least ten minutes. Have your notebook and pen nearby.

2. Seat yourself in a comfortable position on a cushion on the floor or in a chair. Close your eyes and begin to take slow, deep breaths as you settle into your seat. Feel yourself settle even more into the cushion or chair. Place your right hand over your heart and your left hand on your belly. Feel your breath rise and fall. Follow your breath in and out with your attention. If your mind wanders, keep returning to your breath. Keep feeling how deeply you can be seated in yourself. When the timer goes off, keep feeling the seatedness and openness—and whatever other sensations have arisen for you. Turn nothing away.

3. Now consider what wants to come through the door. What have you been wanting to write about that eludes you? Let it be present. If it's dark or difficult to name, settle some more, feel yourself seated and grounded, and ask: What's knocking at my door? Jot

down whatever arises. Maybe it's an image or an idea or a dream or something you want to describe. What is it?

4. Drop your attention to your belly again. Relax your heart. Take a deep breath and exhale loudly. Look at what arose. Turn toward it. Let yourself feel all you need to feel here as you face what wants to come through the door. If your heart is racing or your breath quickens or you want to run away, take note of the accompanying sensations, but don't turn away. Instead, stay with what you're feeling and keep grounding yourself as you face what wants to come through. Be moved by what wants to move through you.

5. Another deep breath. Now extend your arms out in front of you, softly. Let your energy move through your arms and out toward what it is you want to say. Feel your ground, your care, your spirit—and allow the words that now want to be spoken or written. Let it happen. Put your pen to the page now. Keep getting out of the way, and let the force of that energy move you to write words you never imagined you could.

11

Writing, a Surrender

*L*earning the art of falling in aikido practice is an eye- and body-opening experience. It's an experience that requires surrender. In the intimate space of facing another body, you learn what it means to come toward your partner with your full energy, in the form of, say, a punch. Then you learn what it feels like to have your partner move around that punch and control your energy with his hand on the crook of your elbow and another at the back of your neck. When he dips down hard from his center, you follow—you surrender to where he wants to take you. As you fall down to the mats, you keep your own energy gathered, your face protected. It helps to be light. When we're heavy like stone, we tend to feel less. When we lighten, we allow. It is then that we can feel the utterly delicious rounded and full sense of surrendering and falling, like an apple from its tree branch when it's ready to be released.

By definition, surrendering is a kind of giving up or giving over. But it's also a powerful move. The surrender of one body to another on the aikido mats is the most exquisite feeling a body can have. Why? Because in this moment of surrender, one that literally means the body falls to the ground, there is a weightlessness to the experience. What occurs has come from a place of such utter trust, with such an openness of heart and spirit, that the fall, the surrendering, has a power to it that one could not possibly sense otherwise. What the body does is to allow the larger energy that is present to move through and the body joins. It is just what needs to happen in that moment.

Much like on the aikido mats, as writers we have to learn to surrender to what finds its way through the door. But to surrender, first you have to know where you are. Poet Jim Harrison wrote, "Finding myself where I already / am is a daily chore."[1] Although a chore, it's such a necessary one to sense before putting pen to the page, before communicating what's in your heart and mind. How do you "find yourself where you already are"?

Having a consistent practice helps. This could be a sitting practice where you plunk yourself down on a cushion, breathe, and stay alive to the present moment. This is finding yourself where you already are. It could be a bike ride where you allow the landscape to move through you, while you feel yourself as part of something larger, where you can sense what arises from breath and the pumping of your legs, where you can feel into what wants to be known as you ride and ride. It could be a centering practice where you contact your length, width, and depth alongside what matters to you about putting your voice out into the world. *Where you already are.* What mood are you in? What dreams did you have? What voice of the critic is alive in you? What despair? What hope? What spirited revelation? All of it. Where you are.

Finding yourself where you already are is the first step toward the surrender that allows language to move through you. The more you are rooted in yourself, the more you can let that self go. It's as if you put your stake in the ground, and then it serves as a lightning rod for all the ideas, visions, dreams, and revelations to find their way into, then out of, you. This rootedness is the first step toward surrendering to what wants and needs to come through. What is writing if not surrender? What is surrender if not letting go and trusting what is greater than yourself to guide, protect, and lead you into what is next? Surrendering is allowing.

If surrender holds within it the sense of giving up or over, what might this mean? Perhaps we are giving up the limited view we have of ourselves. We are giving over to the idea that there is an energy, a flow, a life force that is always present. What we are yielding to is the idea that we can clear ourselves enough to become a vessel that allows that energy to move through us into language.

What does it mean to create from a place of surrender? It means becoming as present as you possibly can to this moment. It means finding yourself where you already are, which means no turning away from any thought or emotion that comes into you. Instead, you surrender to it. Trust that what occurs to you is exactly what needs to occur to you. It's your thread. It will take your writing (and you) where you must go.

 ## Practice This
Surrendering to What's at Your Door

You've done some exploring about what wants to come through the door. Let's revisit this and take it to another level by practicing what it might mean to surrender to it. When you surrender to what wants to be expressed through you, it changes not only your own perspective but that of your readers. Perhaps you can readily conjure situations in your own life or writing where you have felt surrender as strength. Maybe you even know what surrender feels like to you or what it reminds you of. Or it may be that the concept is strange to you. That's fine. You can choose to play with the concept of surrender itself in this practice if it's giving you trouble. Again, have your notebook and pen nearby.

1. Stand and settle yourself by taking several deep breaths, feeling your feet on the ground and the energy moving down through your legs and into the earth. Align head, heart, and hara into that luminous column. You may even want to gently touch your head at the crown or the third eye, then touch your heart, and then place your hand on your hara. Let the presence of each center settle you some more. Feel, don't think.

2. Go to the door in your space. If it's not directly in your space, find a closed door. Approach the door with curiosity. You might even open the door a crack. Stand and feel and listen. Ask yourself again what wants to come through the door. Listen some more.

3. What have you discovered wants to come through the door? Speak aloud what you're noticing now.

4. If there's nothing that comes, consider how you feel about surrender, what it feels like, what it reminds you of. If surrender itself is a difficult concept, stay with that. What about surrender is hard for you?

5. How is your body responding either to what wants to come through the door or to surrender? Describe what you are sensing and feeling.

6. Whatever you are sensing, stay present with the energy that the idea or concept is giving you. What is it like to stay with either surrender itself or what wants to come through the door? What is the energy or concept saying to you?

7. If you feel at all pressured or uncentered or triggered, return to the breath and the luminous column. Find yourself where you already are. There is no right or wrong about your response—it is simply what is.

8. Sit down at your writing desk. If you are feeling weighted in any fashion, do several two-steps in your writing dojo. Let the two-step bring joy and lightness to your entire body-mind.

9. Pick up your pen or pencil. With lightness and breath, without turning away from your given subject, find yourself where you are and meet your topic with all of yourself as you write for ten minutes, discovering what your relationship is to what met you at your door or to surrendering.

12

Ways of Naming

*A*s writers—and as human beings—we need to live in two places at once: the mysterious and the mundane. The mundane is the daily life we move in—of the world, of the earth. But oftentimes mystery calls to us from somewhere beyond our ken—maybe through our daydreams or night dreams or our intuitive glimpses or the way light shines on an object and gathers our attention. One place isn't necessarily better than the other; we embrace both to find our way.

Sometimes we have to be very specific, name what we're seeing and feeling, go deeper than our first creative impulse so we can take our readers or listeners along with us. And other times we're feeling our way in the dark, more intuiting what it is we must say by feeling into the subject at hand. Both ways of naming—intuiting and specificity—are essential.

We have to see and feel what we're naming. It's not a matter of taking a long trek and coming to a mountain and feeling that because you're the first person to see that mountain, you can name it whatever you please. You have to consider what the mountain might call itself. Naming the mountain doesn't make you feel it more. You have to enter the mystery of the mountain, dig in and create an experience of that mountain beside its name. We need the detail of the naming, yes. But beside that detail, we need the felt sense of our experience just as much.

We need to feel the upward pull of the mysterious beside the downward thrust of the earthly. In fully feeling both places, we can fully see, name, and enter into the experience we are translating through our writing. The world is made rich by the particular. And the ways in which language finds us or we find language is mysterious. We have to enter the mystery of language as if diving into a sea: you don't know what you will find there, but you feel the tug of something underneath the surface.

But how do we hold both places that seem so divergent? On the one hand to feel and to translate emotion into language, and on the other hand to embrace specificity so that what we feel can ripple out into other minds and hearts. One way we do this is by making images. We help someone else to see what we see by giving them a specific image to look through. This creates a concrete way for a reader to enter into the same emotional territory with us. As much as possible, we have to be willing to be clear as we embrace the mystery. Making images of what we see and feel can help another stand beside us.

The language of images is the language of sensation. Images are often visual, but of course they can also be olfactory, tactile, kinesthetic, auditory, or taste related. As we meet the world, we provide pictures in language that translate that meeting. We get specific. We describe what we feel, which is often mysterious, in language that brings those feelings down to earth in the form of images.

One of my first poetry teachers gave me a gift many years ago, which was to show me how the abstractions in a poem, even though deeply felt by me, were not translating into powerful language that a reader could experience. She gave me the assignment of coming up with concrete images for each abstraction. What this made me do was to dig into territory in myself that I had not seen clearly. Such digging required me to ask harder questions and to attempt to define emotional territory with details that could both define and enlarge that territory. It made the writing come alive for me and for the reader. We want to give our readers every chance to stand beside us and to enter into the physical world through our imaginations. Images help us to do just that.

Practice This

Naming the Mysterious and the Mundane with Your Body

Translating what you see and feel by being very specific in your image-making, and also calling on your intuition to guide you deeper, can be quite challenging territory. This practice brings your body into play and helps you first to feel your way into the unknown, then to bring that down to earth in the form of your own way of naming.

1. Begin standing. Place your left foot about a foot in front of your right, in an easy stance with your knees gently bent.

2. Now reach your left arm upward, fingertips pointing to the heavens. As you do this, let yourself settle more in your legs and feet so that you feel supported.

3. Let the elbow of your left arm bend slightly as you play with what it feels like to extend energy through your arm and out the tips of your fingers. Keep breathing.

4. As you are doing this, take note of how your right arm and hand feel down by your side. Don't worry about doing anything just yet, just notice.

5. Now, returning to the left arm in its upward trajectory, imagine that you are extending energy toward the mysterious heavens way above you in territory you know nothing about. Let your arm and hand extend as you ground yourself even more through your legs.

6. Ask: What of the mystery wants to make itself known to me? Give yourself time. Close your eyes as you feel, if that helps you.

7. Write down anything that comes to you here.

8. Now drop your left arm down to its side. Let all that go.

9. Keeping your feet just as they are, with your left foot in front of your right, let your right arm and hand go heavy. Once again, feel your feet on the earth and your legs supporting you. Let the breath freely come and go. Open your hand and have your palm facing down toward the earth. Exhale forcefully as you extend your energy now through that hand and down toward the earth. It's as if you're rooting your hand to the earth through that energetic force field.

10. Close your eyes; breathe in and out slowly and feel the energy of that rooted hand. Imagine what you're up to now is extending energy toward the mundane or earthly. You could look at this as your naming a particular spot on earth as your own. Feel that.

11. Now ask yourself: How would I name or give an image to the mystery that came to me as my left arm was extending toward the heavens? What is the name of that mystery? How do I bring that down to earth right here, right now? Write down any image or particular attribute that surfaces for you.

12. Shake all that out. Take a little walk around your space. You might lightly hold these two ways of naming within you as you walk—the mysterious and the mundane.

13. Now bring yourself back to that posture of left foot comfortably in front of right, hands down at your sides.

14. Now raise your left arm upward again as your right hand reaches downward. Take a few breaths here as you let yourself feel both the upward and downward tug at once.

This figure shows the full engagement of the left arm and hand reaching upward, energy extended toward the heavens, and the right arm and hand extending downward, energy extended toward the earth.

15. If you're feeling adventuresome, step forward with your right leg, raising your right arm now and dropping your left. Again, feel the energy of both upward and downward. Again, step now with your left foot and raise that arm again, while the right drops. You can walk around your space doing this and feeling the differing energies for as long as you wish.

16. Let's write now. As much as you can, keep alive what you were just feeling as you joined the two forces within yourself, the mysterious and the mundane.

17. Take five to ten minutes to write. Begin with one of the mysteries that came to you as you did the above practice. (If none came, then begin with an abstraction, any abstraction—love, longing, resignation, frustration, sorrow, joy.) Write whatever that is across the top of your page. Remembering the feeling you had within you as you moved in your space, creating the mysterious and the mundane with your body, begin to weave the two in your writing. Find concrete particulars—or fluid ones!—that help to define your mystery or your abstraction.

    Remember the richness that comes from naming particulars. Let yourself feel both the mysterious and the mundane. Bring your piece down to earth by being as specific as you can in your naming. If an abstraction wants to remain, if something mysterious calls to you, let this happen, knowing that the abstractions or the mysteries are now supported by the particular.

18. When you're finished writing, read your piece aloud as you walk around your space. What's different about your writing now?

13
The Dance of Listening

*W*riting isn't really recording what we know: it's finding ways to hear what we don't know and getting that down on paper. When we write, we're listening to what wants to be said. We are feeling into language more than rationally deciding what the next right word is. We feel into how the words might connect with each other, how they want to live beside each other, or not. When we listen, we're open to what wants to come through us despite our agendas.

Listening is a dance between what is happening deep within ourselves and what is in our surroundings. Whether we're listening within or without, silence is the requirement. We listen to another by quieting ourselves, putting aside our own desire to speak, and just letting ourselves take in another's words. We listen within ourselves by finding that same space of silence and waiting.

Listening is receiving, and we need to be settled to receive. I had a client who wanted to learn how to settle more deeply within herself so that she could increase her ability to listen, and hear, her poems arise. She did this in two ways: one was to have a sitting practice to help her settle into herself and to pay attention from the inside out. The other was to read a poem before sitting, one that represented the level of passion she wanted to achieve in her own work.

The more open you are, the more acute is your ability to listen. Consider when your heart is open and you have an intimate conversation, how much more is possible. Consider when your belly is open and you need to speak a difficult truth, how much more likely it is that this truth will be available to you. From this sense of openness, you see another and you see yourself with much more accuracy.

Practice This
Listening from a Settled State of Being

As you enter into this dance of listening, paying attention to what is going on both inside and outside of yourself, you can expand your capacity for listening. This practice will help you begin to know how you react, and what happens in your body-self as you react. Then you will settle yourself and see how such settling affects your ability to listen to language anew.

1. Find a brief piece of writing that disturbs you—your own or another's—and bring it with you into your writing dojo. Choose a piece that's a paragraph long or less.

2. As you walk into your space, find a place to stand and read the piece aloud. Let the words reverberate in the air for a few seconds; sink into the disturbed feelings the writing elicits, and then put the writing aside.

3. Now find yourself in a comfortable seated position. Set a timer for five minutes.

4. Gently close your eyes and place your hands on your knees so that your palms are open to the sky. Settle into your seat. Begin to breathe rhythmically in and out to the same beat, at least three seconds each for your inhale and exhale. When your mind clutches onto something or wanders, just notice that and return to your rhythmic breath.

5. When the timer goes off, slowly open your eyes and stay seated for a few seconds more after you turn it off.

6. Now pick up the piece of writing again. Tell yourself you want to listen to the words anew, from your new state. Then read the piece aloud again, slowly savoring each word. Again, let yourself feel how the words affect you.

7. What do you now know about this piece of writing? What is different about it? What is the same? What did you learn by settling and listening?

As we listen from center, we settle more in ourselves, and we act more from center than from all that is constantly tugging at us or disturbing us in some manner. We begin to release our fears, our sense of having to get it right, our expectations, and even our ambitions as we learn to follow the energy of what is present. We can practice our way into receiving rather than pushing.

This kind of listening brings us to territory outside rational thought. If we get quiet and still enough, what can occur then is that a word pops in. When words come in this manner, they are often just right because they're intuited. The seeing of intuition is direct, hits us at a level that is underneath the surface, and is a kind of seeing that is apart from rational thought. But how are we doing this? And further, how can we call upon the powers of intuition as we need them?

As you increase your ability to be receptive and to listen, the words that arise might lead you to a memory or a snapshot of a scene, or the surprise might come in the form of a single image. In a state of receptivity, it is more likely you'll see connections that weren't there before. During this highly intuitive process, there might be an insight—something arises that was not evident before the words began to relate to each other. What arises is often surprising and seems to happen suddenly.

But where does this knowing come from? How do we make intuition more available to us as writers? Focusing is a critical skill to having insights. The focus that's required to get anything at all onto the page leads me to believe that focus is a crucial aspect of awakening to insights. But it's not a laser kind of focusing. It's a soft focus. A soft focus literally opens up your peripheral vision. If we're too driven, if our vision is too one pointed, everything narrows and we don't see what might be waiting just at that periphery to be noticed and experienced. It's as if there's a world out there, yes, but we have to train ourselves to be able to see as much of it as we possibly can—not straight on but peripherally, with a soft focus, with the eyes of dreaming.

A relaxed state encourages intuition, and daydreaming comes from this state. What comes to you as you recline in a hot bubble bath might be very different from what emerges sitting down at your desk at the exact same time every day and making yourself write five pages. Of course, we all have to find our own way with this—there's nothing wrong with a routine around writing. But as with everything else we do, if we get too tight with it, we not only cease to enjoy the task, we also make fewer insightful connections.

As with focus, daydreaming can also be taken to an extreme and become not very useful to writing. We can get lost in it. It's like the difference between a centered state of being and a collapsed state. When we're centered, we're present, open, and connected to ourselves, others, and our environment, while also being relaxed. Sometimes people confuse this state with collapse—when they decide it's time to relax and go slump on the couch with a good drink in hand, for example. But centered isn't collapsed: it's actually utter aliveness to what's inside ourselves as well as to the world around us—an alert attention. We're awake to insights that want to find us.

 ## Practice This
Increasing Your Ability to Receive

As you train yourself to settle and listen, and to receive rather than push, your ability to trust what arises increases, too. As your ability to center in yourself increases, you become more alive and awake to insights. Here's a way to practice listening so that you can weave words into a new shape.

Listening Within

1. Stand facing a blank wall. Settle, close your eyes, and place your right hand over your heart. Take six deep breaths, settling yourself even more.

2. Ask yourself and listen: What are the five words that I am feeling right now?

3. As the words arrive, repeat them to yourself. As each new word arrives, repeat the growing list of words until you have your five.

4. Now write those five words down.

Listening Without

1. Stand facing open space. Give yourself enough room to accomplish a two-step in that space. With eyes open, place one foot in front of the other to prepare to two-step. (I think you know this move by now, if you've been practicing all along in the book, but refer to chapter 6 if you need a refresher.) Hold your arms out so that your palms are facing upward. As you begin to two-step, keep this posture of having your palms up so that you can feel what it's like to receive as you move.

2. Two-step at least four times.

3. Then on the next round, ask yourself: What are the five words that my environment is speaking to me right now?

4. Again, as the words arrive, repeat them to yourself aloud. Repeat the growing list of words until you have your five.

5. Then write these five words down.

Blending Your Listening

1. Sit down at your writing desk with pen and paper and your ten words.

2. Spend time with your words, first looking at and feeling into the five that arrived from deep within you. Then bring the five that came from your surroundings into your present awareness.

3. Now take up your pen and begin to write, choosing one word, then the next, as inspiration for a brief, timed writing. Write for ten minutes, weaving both lists of words, seeing and feeling how the words want to relate to each other, as well as what else might arise as you join words that you may have never put together before. Let yourself be surprised, even delighted, at the new language you're making.

14

Bringing Your Body
to the Page

*W*hen is it that we feel the most open to the life we're living? There are many answers to this question, given we are many-faceted human beings. On first blush, though, I'd say that we can be most open when we're most trusting. When we're not defensive. When we laugh. When we love. When we're less concerned about what people will think of us than with our desire and right to express ourselves. When we're fully engaged with what's in front of us. When we can get out of our own way. When we can give ourselves over.

Of course, all of this applies to your life as a writer, too. To be able to encounter the blank page over and over again with more and more of yourself, you have to develop a trusting relationship both with your writer-self and with your writing. A relationship that matches the best of human relationships you've had—one that contains great waves of love in it.

As with many complexities, there is no formula here. Your writing and your writer-self operate in tandem. To deepen your relationship with one is to alter the other. I recall a practice a client devised so that she could become more fully cognizant of and aligned with her body moving in space. Why? So that she could create the ground under herself as she moved. She would simply go for a walk in the English countryside, what she named "walking the dale." She could feel what it meant to her body-self to create that ground and to trust that it was there with her every step. She could bring more and more of herself to that ground the more she trusted her own deepening presence on that ground. Occupying that ground with all of herself began to transform her relationship to her writing. The ground of the dale and the ground of the page were one and the same. She transformed her relationship to both.

Maybe you already have a strong sense of the ground your writing occupies, but you notice that you often feel your voice is not your own, that when you write there's a kind of smokescreen that appears. Yet what you most want is to get to the heart of the matter. You want your writing to express vulnerability and strength in equal measure. You want to speak the truth, but that's terrifying and pretty uncomfortable, and anyway, you don't know how. What if your body could tell you how? What might that look like?

Let's say that you notice constriction in your hips and a tendency to lean back when someone else gets too close to you. You see and feel these things, but what you want is to feel fluidity when you're dancing (or writing) and to be able to stand strongly facing another, even when the other is close in. You can reveal yourself to yourself through noticing how you are in differing situations of your life or in your practices. And then you can practice something new. You can commit to a new way of being, which will in turn change your relationship to both yourself and your writing.

Hula hooping. Singing. Circling your hips as you listen to your favorite music. Building your capacity to feel yourself differently also builds your ability to access your deepest voice. As we learn how to soften the tight spots and thaw what's been frozen within us, we come into our own—both in body and in language. The more we practice something new, the more we can gain access to places in ourselves that have been shut off. Initially as you practice an open-hipped stance, you might feel uncomfortable and exposed, but the more you practice, the more you gain access to that power, to your ground and to your center—as well as to your heart. If we can't be fully with ourselves and willing to expose what is hidden deep within, how can our words affect others?

What is your real language, the language that originates from deep inside yourself that could then resonate with other people? Honing what is true for you and what is not helps you name the ground you walk on. Feeling your own balance and strength, alongside a lower center of gravity, helps you to feel your own gravitas. You can expand your capacity to be exactly where you are and to be with what is. As you continue on the path of unearthing your truest voice—improper, witty, intelligent, fiery, bright—you'll unearth, too, your truest self. Through body-centered work you can feel beyond the usual limitations or past structures you've lived in. As you learn more and more how to inhabit your vulnerability, how to be with whatever arises, you will keep creating the sacred time required to write. You'll learn how to ask: How do I keep uncovering my excitement?

And your writing will begin to take shape from the new shape you are becoming. Who wouldn't want to keep showing up for that kind of relationship?

Practice This
Accessing Your Voice from the Inside

Consider and write about the following questions.

1. What is your current relationship with your writing?
2. How would you characterize your relationship with your writer-self?
3. In terms of either relationship, where do you notice yourself tightening or constricting? What does this feel like and look like?
4. Whatever you've named above, choose a quality that you would like to develop or deepen in yourself or your writing life. Say the quality aloud.
5. Take this quality for a walk. Each step that you take, let this quality be the huge ground beneath you. As you step, speak the quality aloud, and as you hear your voice speaking, let that voice reverberate down your legs, into your feet, and into the earth. Walk with your quality until you sense you are actually getting to know what

this feels like all through you. What does it feel like and look like to own this quality now?

6. Now describe this quality as if your audience has no clue as to what it is. If your quality is, say, love, then your readers know nothing of love. Tell them what it is with as much detail and feeling as you can.

7. Next put on some of your favorite dancing music. Give yourself some space. Dance, wiggle, circle your hips, jump up and down, let yourself move in whatever way your quality is speaking to you. Shake your shoulders. Do figure eights with your hips. Move your head. Let yourself be fluid. Take a good five minutes with your dance.

8. Now write about your quality again in the same manner as above. What do you have to say now about your quality? Go!

9. What did you discover about the nature of your real language? How can you speak your own truth? How does your body inform you?

15

The Companion Energy
of Support

One of the many ways in which we can increase our sense of belonging and relaxation is to let ourselves feel supported. By this I don't mean just listing the people in your life who are on your side, although that's a start. For support to effectively assist our work, we have to feel it throughout our soma.

When we feel supported, it is often easier to align with what we care about and to move forth with more aplomb. Feeling support, letting it enter us, can help us to feel more grounded and write from a more centered, spirited, open place in ourselves. Support, actual and felt, can help us embrace our vulnerability alongside that of others and express the energy and wit of our true voice.

One client I had was stretching herself to feel support more directly. One thing she did was to make a poster of her ideal readers—these included real people who had told her they wanted to read her book. As she practiced writing while feeling her readers literally at her back, she felt her ability to connect with the interests of her readers increase. She said she suddenly had a deep sense of ease about her writing along with the realization that there was no place else to go but into the work. As she became more and more able to let in support, she literally felt her body become more porous. Within that realization and sensation, she was both herself and everyone. She felt this enabled her to write from her heart.

To be able to feel support, first it helps to identify the qualities of the support you need. Maybe the support you need is to know you're loved, that your work is appreciated. Maybe it's that you want to have your work read critically. Maybe you want your readers to tell you they are intrigued by your subject matter. Maybe you just need to read your work aloud to someone else and have that person smile, without comment.

As you create your circle of support, ask what you need beside you or at your back to feel you are in deep communion with an energy you could name your companion energy. Your companion energy could be one person, or it could be that circle, or it could be a feature in the landscape. Within your coterie, create the wide-ranging support you require. That could mean you choose a writer you admire. You might choose a mountain, an ocean, a river, a field. As you consider what strengths you want to bring to your writing, think about those you know or know of who already possess what you desire. Bring all of this into your circle.

Practice This
Identifying Qualities of Support

To help you define and unearth the ways in which you feel supported, consider the following questions, writing answers to them in your notebook.

1. Whose life speaks to you, moves you, or inspires you?
2. What in the natural landscape has made you feel most deeply supported?
3. What kind of support would make you feel excited about your writing?
4. What do you need someone to say to you so that you feel deeply supported?
5. What are the qualities of your ideal readers?
6. Name as many ideal readers as you can, people who already support you.

As you consider what your own version of support would look like, also imagine that you could evoke your circle of supporters at any time and enter your writing space as sacred space, bringing them along with you. Experiment with feeling into your circle of supporters and seeing how this affects your writing output and the spirit with which you share your work. As you ask for support and bring others along with you, remember to hold strongly to your own vision and voice. Let your coterie help you deepen that vision and voice.

Having companion energy that you can call on at any time helps you to soften. When you soften, you will see changes. As you change the way you organize your energy by letting in support, you will change the way you think about your work. Then you'll be able to extend your own energy more powerfully into the work at hand in your own inimitable way.

 Practice This
Increasing Your Felt Sense of Support

Having identified qualities of support you need as well as possible members of your circle of support, let's experiment with a few ways of feeling that support.

Creating a Collage of Support

1. One way to bring your circle into your writing dojo is to create a collage of its members. You can do this by gathering photographs or other images of your coterie. Then put them together in a way that satisfies you and have this collage readily available for your viewing. If it's ideal readers that would help you feel supported, make a poster with their names and photographs and keep this near you in your writing space. Remember these can be people you know, or they can be writers you admire or teachers you've loved.

2. Before you begin to write, look at the collage or poster and relate to each person or landscape in the images. Remember who they are to you; let yourself feel their energy and the support they bring

you. Stand in your writing dojo, center yourself in that space, and turn toward your companions. Pay attention to how your heart feels. Then how your gut feels.

3. Notice anything that shifts in you as you let in your circle of support. What do you notice? What happens in you as you turn toward your circle and let all of it touch you?

Opening the Back Body

Another way to increase your ability to feel supported is to open your back body. This isn't always easy or simple, but you can try a few things to help you open more. What we're opening to is that sense of being supported, of being able to feel, literally, what's at our backs, to let in that support.

1. If you have an exercise ball, you can practice feeling the shape of your back opening by lying back on the ball. This also opens your chest, as you'll see. Play with moving around the ball by adjusting where your back rests on the ball. Find a comfortable spot and then spend a minute or two allowing yourself to feel the sensation of openness and support simultaneously.

2. What do you notice as you do this? What's it feel like to let support into your back?

3. If you don't have an exercise ball, find a tree that you love. Walk up to the tree trunk, turn around, and let your whole back body press against the trunk. Feel the support of the tree enter your back body. Feel your ground. Then open your arms wide and take several deep breaths. Let yourself feel your ground, your open arms and chest, and your back body, all supported by the tree.

4. What do you notice as you do this? What does it feel like to let support into your back body?

Tapping into Companion Energy

And finally, tapping into your particular companion energy as you need to will move you more deeply into your strengths and energetic offering. As your strengths and energetic offerings evolve, your companion energy may change. What or who best represents your companion energy now?

1. Stand facing the inside of an imaginary circle. You are part of its outer edges. Feel the circle's edge fill up with all those you would place beside you on this writing journey. Who supports you? You don't have to know these others, or you might. Create the circle with all you have or can imagine at your back. Let yourself look around the circle at these supporting humans. Look into everyone's eyes. Feel the support they offer you. Maybe there's one person in your group who is a particular companion energy for you. Nod to this person. Ask them to stand beside you and place a hand at your lower back. You do the same for them. Let their support into your back body. Let it settle you. Let it enter your heart and gut and lungs.

2. Now take at least ten minutes and free-write about your companion energy and how you can continue to welcome a depth of support into your writing, your life.

Part Three

Turning Obstacles into Doorways

▶ Come to know your historic patterns so that you can see what they offer you and how you can step over the threshold they provide and enter into new territory.

▶ Explore what doubt feels like through your body.

▶ Experience how fear can be transformed into courage as you face the blank page.

▶ Discover how naming your own darkness can help you to embody your writing with complexity and fullness.

▶ Look at the ways of your own hiding and see its effect on your use of language; as you work with feeling yourself more and more, you'll find ways to express the full range of your emotions and trust your own voice.

▶ Find your way through your own cycles of order and disorder and discover the relationship between messiness and vibrancy.

16

The Doorway of Our Histories

The aikido dojo is a powerful place of transformation. Your writing dojo can be that, too—a place where you learn to feel and blend with the energy of the other. In aikido once practitioners learn to feel the energy of another body, they can learn to redirect what might otherwise be construed as an attack and to neutralize the oncoming energy. We each need to enter our dojo with what my sensei once called "an empty cup." No preconceived notions about what might occur. Not even any preconceived idea about who we are. What stops learning is to enter the dojo thinking we have all the answers. You have to be willing to just show up and train—or write. Willingness gets you across the threshold. When you are willing to engage with what shows up, say, as you move through your days or wrestle with words on the page, then you can make immediate shifts in body consciousness that create a new way of seeing, being, moving, or doing. Awareness does lead to choice.

We all have historic patterns that are invisible to us and that may prevent us from letting out the full range of our voice and vision. Bringing awareness to these patterns is the first step. And then we have to open to the possibility of another way of acting, another way of being. These historic patterns are tendencies that, over time, have become embodied. These moments of our shaping are defining moments. Inside the events that happen in our lives, we respond with all of our intelligence. We learn what we need to do. We ask ourselves, even if unconsciously: What is the shape I need to be in to feel safe? To connect to those in my sphere? To know my value? Once we surface these deeply held patterns alongside the emotions and beliefs that are integral to them, we can begin to choose another way.

If we can put ourselves to the task of surfacing what is invisible (as much of writing is), then we can work with the patterns we find within us, celebrate the ones that are working for us, and have the choice to change the ones that are not. As an example, I once worked with what one of my clients named the "habit of effort." That this pattern was alive in me was shown to me by an aikido sensei who mirrored my technique, showing me that I was relying heavily on my biceps. This led to an inability to move my partner because I was tightening or using effort rather than joining or flowing. Not only did I see it, I *felt* it, and I understood that I was holding on to a belief that I held to be sacrosanct: that I had to work really hard to get anywhere. I had assumed this belief was true, but it wasn't. As that sensei said: "You don't *need* your biceps!"

Once I knew what the way of effort felt like in my own body, I could then take my attention, imagination, and spirit of inquiry off the mats and into my writing and life. Shifting my focus from bicep to belly, dropping my attention from the effort of bicep to the knowing of belly, awakened my curiosity. What happens if I let go of my mind's intent to move my partner and instead join my partner's desire to be moved? What if I stop worrying about what it is I want to write and just sit down, listen, and join the writing that wants to be written?

Off the mats, in my writing and in my life, I kept asking: What if instead of trying and tightening I loosen and let be? During this inquiry, as I practiced letting go of strain, I would catch myself applying unneeded effort for even the most mundane tasks—such as making pesto and straining to release the basil leaves from their stems. Once noticed, once surfaced, I could shake off the effort and realize I didn't need it. Once released, a different kind of seeing replaced the effort; my senses came alive. I felt more able to move through my days with grace rather than difficulty.

Underneath the habit of effort is fear, all the ways we can constrict ourselves and stop the flow of aliveness from moving through us. Maybe you don't believe you can keep showing up to the blank page. Maybe you don't feel supported or feel what your place on earth is, how you belong. All this can lead right into the habit of effort. And you can keep trying—to show up when you write, to know more and more, to belong—but these efforts don't lead us to write more truly or fearlessly. When we're applying effort, we are not centered. Head, heart, and hara are not aligned. We create a blockage rather than a flow. There's also judgment in effort: we can look at our writing, for instance, as a thing of beauty one day and the next the same piece can cause us consternation. We can learn how to let go of effort and root ourselves instead in the silence beneath. We can learn to have conviction in our work rather than fear of what we might say. We can learn to believe in what we're up to as writers as we learn to let go of trying so damn hard.

We're shining a light on what challenges us here. You may have many ways of being or historic patterns that serve you and your writing; that's great. But you may also find that because of a particular pattern and belief you find it difficult to get words down on paper, or read your work in public, or have your words match your heart, or stop comparing yourself with others, or fear being ridiculed, or feel ungrounded, or fear being visible. The list is endless!

Yet we can't get rid of this shaping—it *is* us. There is always a positive aspect to our patterns. If being quiet and going inward is a historic pattern you have, maybe this allowed you to become the writer you've become. Rather than trying to be something else, we accept what we see that we are. And as we disentangle from what has been historically true for us, we begin to feel a possibility emerge that gives us more options—more aliveness, more of a sense of our own potential. We make new meaning.

The more we can make visible what challenges us and grapple with the challenge until we feel and understand it, the freer we will be as writers and creative beings, and the more we will open to and be inspired by the words that want to find their way through us.

 *Practice This*

Identifying Your Historic Patterns

What are your historic patterns that you may not even be aware of right now? Let's play with ways to surface your invisibles.

Consider the following questions. Choose the ones to engage with that speak to you most strongly.

1. When you are faced with a blank page or some time to really engage with your creative work, what prevents you? What are you telling yourself over and over? Take five minutes to write down every voice that arises as you consider this.

2. When you sit down to write, what's the trouble you can get into? What makes you stuck or unable to write? What's the loudest voice in your ears? Take five minutes to write down what arises as you consider this.

3. Take a day, or several, in which you pay attention to when you feel pressure—this can be internal questioning or it can come from external sources. Jot down what that pressure says to you, what it feels like, what it has you believe about yourself or your writing.

4. Consider when you are startled or surprised by something or someone. What do you notice in your body-self when you are knocked off your center? Choose a real-life circumstance or encounter and take ten minutes to write down what shakes you up and what happens in your body and beliefs in these circumstances.

5. When you are not pleased with your writing or writing output or when you're not feeling in the flow of your writing, what do you notice about your body posture or sensations? Write down all that you're experiencing.

 Practice This

A Somatic Experience of Your Pattern

Review your answers to the questions in the practice above. Ask yourself what keeps showing up in your answers or what is the strongest pattern living in you. Choose one of those above patterns or situations to explore somatically. Ask yourself these questions and answer in writing.

1. What is the shape your body is making as you feel into this pattern? What does it feel like? Does an image arise around this feeling in your body? What's the temperature, texture, or color of this sensation in your body? What images arise as you let yourself feel your pattern deeply?

2. What is the belief attached to this particular shaping or pattern? Take some time to consider what the gift of this pattern is. How has it helped you be who you are?

3. Become really intimate with this new awareness. Sit with what you've written down. Read it aloud, and let it circle you. Let yourself recognize how this pattern lives in you and the shape or posture it creates in your body. Consider, too, what this pattern or posture has you believe about yourself.

4. When this pattern has you in its grip, what's the shape your body makes? Get into this shape and exaggerate it. Stay in this exaggerated shape for at least twenty seconds. What's the shape look like? What do you feel? What are you thinking?

5. Deepen into this shape even more and ask: What is this shape protecting? Let yourself feel the ways in which this shaping has served you. You might even feel moved to thank this shaping for what it's given you.

6. Then ask the shape what it would like to turn into now. Let yourself feel this as a possibility.

7. Now bring the rest of you to the awareness of this new shape. Stand up. Drop your attention into your hara or belly and breathe from there. Exaggerate your inhale, really taking in a lot more breath than you usually allow yourself. Then just let your exhale out in one swoosh. Keep this up for ten breaths and then just see how you feel, what you're noticing.

8. Now place your attention on your legs. What do you notice? Can you feel your feet on the ground? Can you extend energy down through your legs into the earth? Try this. Notice what shifts in you.

9. Soften your heart. Ask yourself what you care about with your writing. How can this new shape help you get where you want to be? What is your deepest desire as you put your voice out into the world or onto the page? Let this reverberate throughout your entire being. Extend the feeling of your care out through your heart. What do you notice now?

10. Now feel into your gut. What do you want to dare to create? How does that feel in your gut? Wherever you feel tightness, bring space there.

11. Keep with this for at least five minutes—breath, legs, heart, gut. Now ask yourself: What do I believe now about my creative work? What do I want to happen next?

12. Again, give yourself time and space to feel this desire throughout your whole being. Again, deep breath, feel your legs, extend out through your heart, let your gut go, and speak aloud what you believe right now about your creative self, about your writing.

Know this. You own this vision for yourself and your work. Take this with you.

Keep practicing. Whenever you feel stuck or frustrated or pressured in any way, take yourself through this process. Be vigilant about your historic patterns so that you know when they surface and also know that you can keep choosing a new way of being over and over.

Rather than living in a state of contraction, you can move more and more toward your aliveness and toward your ability to fully express yourself out of that aliveness.

17

The Doorway of Doubt

There are two kinds of doubt that often arise the deeper we stride into the writing arena. They are quite distinct. One is debilitating. One is necessary. The first I would call self-doubt; the second, creative doubt. These two doubts often dance with each other as we attempt to make things happen on the page.

Writing often brings up the terrain of self-trust and self-doubt. You have to have a bedrock of belief in your own perspective and experience to write anything at all. When this bedrock is shaky, your self-doubt makes you question everything, even your own existence. You might doubt that you belong. You might doubt you have anything of worth to say. You might doubt that your words, if you do manage to say anything, could have any effect at all. You might doubt your intelligence, your wisdom, your writing ability. You might doubt that you know how to write a poem or a paragraph, or that you can communicate what matters to you. This can be as true for someone who has published several books as it is for the new writer.

Of course, self-doubt is debilitating. Disruptive. It doesn't allow us to find even a few words, let alone a sense of flow as those words form sentences, stanzas, speeches, or any heartfelt correspondence. Self-doubt is like a braking system that's gone awry—there we are driving along smoothly and the car starts to jerk. By questioning the worth of what we might have to say, we prevent ourselves from discovering what that might be.

Practice This
The Mask of Self-Doubt

Let's identify your own particular version of self-doubt with this imaginative practice.

1. First do some brainstorming on paper about your version of self-doubt. What is the flavor of your self-doubt? What does it look like, feel like? Is it that you don't know enough, you don't think you can make a difference, or you're worried something awful will occur if you reveal yourself in your writing? Do you compare yourself to others and come up short? Are you obsessed with perfection?

2. Now imagine that you are putting on a mask that represents the shape and face of your self-doubt. What does that mask look like? Does it cover only your face or more than that?

3. Put the mask on. Notice how you feel with the mask on your body. Walk around your writing dojo with your mask on and feel what the mask allows and doesn't allow.

4. Now take the mask off. Notice anything that happens in your body or your thoughts. Write for at least five minutes about what you understand now about your version of self-doubt—what it feels like to have it on, and then what it's like to remove it. What becomes possible for you when the mask of your self-doubt is put aside?

5. Ask yourself how you might refute or counter each self-doubt that's arisen. Come up with statements that show what's not true about each self-doubt. Go wild and come up with statements that make you laugh, they're so outrageously not you.

When dealing with our self-doubts, the only way is *through*. It takes desire, persistence, and maybe even stubbornness to keep at it and to face into whatever our self-doubts are. Over time, they do quiet down. We must name them, be diligent in noticing when they arise, and counter them with something wiser, something truer. Something new will come into being because you've persisted.

Creative doubt occupies an entirely different territory and expresses itself in the body differently than self-doubt. Creative doubt is generative. Creative doubt helps us to refine what it is we want to say and to dive back into original text to make it better. Creative doubt helps us re-vision our work. Creative doubt is tender, is not self-righteous, listens deeply, questions sharply, makes us better writers (and probably better partners, collaborators, etc.).

Creative doubt helps us to refine our voices, make them truer. When we're in the state of creative doubt, we are not doubting our creative urges or necessity; we're able to employ objectivity. We face into the work at hand and are able to make creative decisions to improve that work. The objectivity of creative doubt is its strength—it allows us to see beyond ourselves. When we exercise creative doubt, we recognize a weakness and are open to turning that weakness into something vital and strong. Creative doubt can actually bring us to certainty.

Creative doubt has a different shape to it. If self-doubt is a mask, then creative doubt is a laser beam. It might wake us up at night with questions about word choice in a piece we're working on and help us to find the right word. Or it might crop up when you read your work aloud and find it bumpy. You're giving yourself some distance from the writing itself as you literally give voice to it, and sometimes this exposes what's not working. We can listen differently to language when it's lifted off the page, and the dissonance helps us to approach the bumpy lines anew and smooth them out. We might become uncertain in these moments, asking: What could make the line sing? But we aren't doubting ourselves. The distance and the objectivity possible in creative doubt makes for a different kind of listening.

Practice This
Exploring Creative Doubt

Let's assume that creative doubt is a laser beam. Take out your laser beam and a piece of writing you've had doubts about and have given up working on. Then try the following steps to help you use your creative doubt to further your writing.

1. Shine your beam on the writing. Feel the sharpness and directed quality of that light. Imagine the beam is coming from inside you.
2. Where does the beam go to in your piece? What is this telling you?
3. Read your challenging piece aloud. Ask the piece itself what wants to

emerge. Is it a different tone? A different word choice? Another form?

4. Engage with your writing as you would a good friend you're having a difficult conversation with—be tender but also be sharp. Assess what is needed, what is required, to bring your writing forth with spirit and aplomb. Use your creative doubt to get you there.

5. How did engaging with creative doubt help you go further with your work?

A woman poet I know was writing a journal on the political state of our union in 2019. I read two of what she named "chapters" of this potential "book." I put these in quotes because, at the time, she was in a state of creative doubt around form and shape and the offering she was making through her writing. It was powerful, compelling, wise work. I wanted it to see the light of day. Her vision, her intelligence, her view of our country at that time of turbulence, where it was hard to tell what was true anymore, were all palpable in her writing. Her version of creative doubt was definitely one of form. Her writing had no self-doubt in it. (She may have her own version of her process, of course, but self-doubt is not what shone through her words.) So, with persistence, with the questions I know she was capable of asking, with tenderness and a depth of listening, she came to what needed to happen with these chapters and this book. Through her own process of creative doubt, her writing found its form.

 ## Practice This
Cutting through Any Kind of Doubt

Sometimes a simple, direct practice can help to move us into a clearer state of being. If you find yourself mired in doubt, simply do this:

1. Hold your right hand perpendicular to the floor, with your little finger downward and your thumb up. Keep your fingers tightly closed. This is your "sword," with your little finger as the sword edge. Open the palm of your left hand and pound the sword edge of your right hand into the palm of your left. Relax for a few seconds. Breathe and settle.

2. Notice how you are feeling, and then try it again.

3. What happens to your doubt or sense of focus? Now what? What is one action you can take from this place of newfound energy or focus?

18

The Doorway of Fear

Often as we write we want to discover something new. We want to engage with language in a way that moves others, that helps us understand something about ourselves and the world we live in that we did not see before. We want to create worlds through language. We want to create beauty through language and bring our thoughts and the shape of our ideas to a larger audience. We seek dialogue. And yet sometimes—maybe all the time—we're afraid.

Sometimes our fear can be based on facing difficult emotions or memories as we write; other times it might be more closely related to the writing at hand and whether we can deal with tackling a certain piece of work, format, or topic. Sometimes fear can surround us without any visible reason, but it's palpable, a kind of free-floating fear.

What is there to be afraid of? We are simply putting pen to paper or typing away on our laptops. We do that all the time—in email correspondence, letters, notes, lists, and often in our work. Why can it cause such consternation? Writing is an activity we've been doing since grammar school. Wouldn't you think it would be an embodied skill by now?

Clearly, it is not an embodied skill for most. By embodied I mean it's something that is so much a part of us that its execution is utterly natural. Interesting word choice: execution. Why does the task of writing sometimes feel like heading to one's own execution? I am only partly joking. We avoid moving that pen along the page because writing can feel like a life-or-death proposition.

Writing is a deep encounter with our thoughts and intellect, our feelings and emotions. There is no avoiding that encounter once you start the pen moving. We want writing that explodes inside us, that changes our emotional landscape, that teaches us something valued and new, that opens doorways to minds and hearts. Why write at all if we don't at least aspire to shake things up, feel with depth and clarity, and spark others to do the same?

No wonder fear can arise when we're faced with the blank page. We don't have any way of knowing what will happen: what words will take shape on the page, what connections we'll make that we were never able to make before, what revelations will occur to us, what questions will arise, what a new way of seeing will do to our lives. Yet we want to write.

Writing happens when we transform fear into courage. Writing fearlessly is writing authentically.

 ## Practice This
Letting the Fear Out

Before we can sit down and write fearlessly, first we have to know what we're afraid of.

1. Sit down at your writing desk, pen in hand, and ask yourself what you are most afraid of. Write all the fears you can think of and feel about yourself, about your writing. As many as you can. Repeat if you need to! Take only five minutes to do this, just make a list, writing quickly. Try to stay out of your own way.

2. In the introduction to this book, I encouraged you to read poems to let them inform you, to let the energy of poetic language into your whole being. Here's a chance to do a little digging and to find this poem centered around fear. The poem is called "Fear," and it's by Raymond Carver. It's in his collection of poems entitled *Where Water Comes Together with Other Water.*[1]

3. Stand in your writing dojo and read Raymond Carver's poem aloud, letting his fears mingle with whatever is inside you in this moment. Let Carver's fears touch your own.

4. If reading Carver's poem aloud reminded you of more fears of your own, add these to your list now.

As in Carver's poem, there are plenty of possibilities for what each of us fears. We often fear both the thing and its opposite. We fear big things, like death, and we fear smaller things, like being late for an appointment or being first to a party. This is likely so with our fears around writing, too.

What can you do? You can look your fears straight in the eye and see what they want of you. After that you can see if there's anything to be done about what our fear is saying and do it. Once you have looked your fear in the eye (fear feels like a cyclops to me), you can choose to find another way to relate to it. But you can only discover this other relationship if you confront, rather than ignore, your fear. When ignored, fear becomes more powerful.

As Buddhist nun and author Pema Chödrön once observed: "Fear is a natural reaction to moving closer to the truth."[2] Anaïs Nin said that "life shrinks or expands in proportion to one's courage."[3] We have to face our fears over and over and use our fears as a measure of getting closer to the bone of our truth. It takes courage to write, to create something out of what appears to be nothing—if nothing is silence, the blank page, the tabula rasa of our very soul. Courage is the container for our wisdom. To stand *in* and *with* ourselves is the first step toward knowing who we are enough to know what it is we want to say. Facing our fear can feel like flinging open a door to the field of our courage where we can frolic for longer and longer periods of time by speaking and writing in our own earned voice.

Practice This
Finding Courage to Face Your Fear

Now that you have a list of your fears, you can practice your way into facing one fear at a time and moving into what is possible as you relate to your fear, finding new ground for your writing.

1. Stand up and feel your feet on the ground. Lift up your arms, one at a time, stretching and reaching each of your fingertips to the heavens. Then let your energy settle back down and feel your ground again.

2. Open your heart by opening your arms wide out to your sides at

chest level. Expand your chest and open and relax your shoulders, no hunching or hunkering down. If this position is new or scary, place your right hand over your heart as you do this. Even if it's not a new sensation for your heart to be open, that hand can feel really good. Now let your arms come back down to your sides at your hips but keep the open feeling in your heart.

3. Now take four deep breaths from your belly and let out a loud exhale or sigh on each one. Just feel yourself in this grounded, open, expanded way.

4. Now imagine a fear that you named earlier is standing to the right of you. Don't look at it yet, just feel it there. Name it out loud: "I am afraid of . . ." Let it touch you.

5. Notice anything that happens in your own body, breath, thoughts, emotions, feelings, sensations. Repeat your fear aloud. Notice again. Make room to let your fear touch you. What is it saying to you? What are you noticing about your own reactions? Let these be.

6. Return to yourself as you did initially through breath, grounding and opening your heart.

7. When you feel ready, turn your body to the right and literally face your fear. Again, let it touch you. If you are experiencing difficulty, expand your sense of ground and heart. Open more, ground more. Let your fear touch you.

8. And now speak what it is you want to say to your fear. Speak it aloud. Speak it from your grounded presence and open heart. Tell it what you need, what you want, who you are as a writer and creative being, whatever comes to you that you need to say. Speak for at least a minute but certainly for much longer if that is what you need.

9. Now sit down and write for at least ten minutes. What is your fear around your writing? What is the nature of the fear that descends on you when you write? What was it like to face that fear? What did you learn in the process of doing so? Is there something that you need to write down on a card to keep at your writing desk to remind yourself of how to talk back to your fear? What becomes possible for you and your writing now?

19

The Doorway of Our Darkness

*W*riting is a kind of forging. We heat and we hammer until what we have is a piece of work. There's alchemy in the process, too. As we surface what has been invisible, we have the chance to meet it, even to transform it.

English writer D. H. Lawrence said: This is what I believe: "That I am I. That my soul is a dark forest. That my known self will never be more than a little clearing in the forest. That gods, strange gods, come forth from the forest into the clearing of my known self, and then go back. That I must have the courage to let them come and go."[1] Writing can help us find our way through that dark forest. But first we have to find out what our darkness is made of. When we write we shine a light on the unknown; we bring light to that place in ourselves that has been a dark forest to us. Our writing is an uncovering, an unveiling, a lustration.

We all have our dark corners. We have to be willing to peer into that dark, as we might have done as a child sneaking a look under the bed. We have to find the courage to name our darkness. What are its elements? Who are its characters? In what ways does the dark keep you quiet, hidden, locked up? In what ways could your dark free you? As writers we bring what is subject to us into the light of objectivity. With our imaginations we transform what is now in the dark to something real that can be touched and felt and acted upon. Making our dark conscious through language brings complexity and fullness to our writing.

Darkness tends to live behind things, underneath things, in the depth of things. We could say that it lives at our backs or in the deeper reaches of our psyches. I remember a client once saying that as she began to feel into her back body, she immediately felt this darkness: "It's dark in my back—not dark in a bad way, but dark as mysterious, as something I could work with in my writing," she said. Another client once wisely noted that as long as she did not find ways to own up to her own secrets, or darkness, her writing would remain outside herself rather than come from her gut and her heart. She wanted to increase her capacity to speak out from her private, rather than her public, self and to do that she knew that her voice, literally, had to come from a different place. She realized that her secrets kept her circling around a topic rather than facing it, digging in, and courageously naming what she saw and felt.

 ## Practice This
Giving Shape to the Unseen

What is unrevealed holds immense power. But we have to find ways to unearth what we can't see. Bringing curiosity to our darkness, to our backs, to what's behind and beneath helps us to fathom how what's unseen might be informing us.

1. Lie on your back comfortably and let yourself feel supported by the floor, mattress, couch, or whatever is beneath you. Take several deep breaths as you close your eyes, feeling into the dark spaces as you also feel that support, and consider the following questions.

   • Who or what from the unseen back of me wants to be known or felt?

   • What words want to be spoken from this unseen place?

   • What's an image that rises from the darkness that wants to be known or remembered right now?

2. Sit up and grab your notebook and pen. Now take five minutes or more to write anything that arose as you asked yourself the above questions. Let what wants to be seen arise as you write. Remember as much as you can what came up as you were lying down, but just let your pen move across the page, revealing what comes to you from your inner dark, that powerful unseen.

 ## Practice This

Increasing Your Ability to Feel What's Behind You

You may have found that in the practice above it was difficult to access anything at all. That's OK. This could be strange and new to you. There are a few ways to increase your ability to feel behind you or to feel into the unseen.

1. You already know one of these practices, the two-step. As you practice your two-step, pay particular attention to your back body as you step and turn. If you feel wobbly or unable to feel your back, before you begin the two-step, imagine you have many hands at your back. Put all the people who support you right there at your back, take a deep breath, and as you exhale feel those hands. Then practice your two-step, filling your back body with energy and consciously expanding the field behind you with your curiosity and inquiry. What wants to be felt there?

2. Another practice to help you feel the field behind you is to slowly and mindfully walk backward. Find a place with plenty of room for you to walk backward without running into anything for at least ten steps. As you begin, place one foot in front of the other in a comfortable stance. Take three deep breaths and feel the ground beneath you. Now place your forward foot behind you slowly and settle again. Repeat this until you've moved mindfully across the space, feeling your back body and the field behind you each step of the way.

When we allow ourselves to feel and express our own places of darkness, we broaden the depth and range of our unique voices. Think of looking up at the night sky with its pinpoints of light. We feel all our senses more acutely as we stand under the blackness of a night sky. If we face our own night sky, the one inside us, the one behind us, we'll see there are pinpoints of light there, too, ones that can illuminate our path forward.

 ## *Practice This*
Accepting What's Behind You

As you begin to identify the qualities of your own darkness, through naming and feeling into it, as you did in the above practices, the next step is to accept that piece of darkness as an integral part of who you are.

1. Stand with your legs hip-distance apart facing an open view, if possible, arms by your side, palms facing forward. Settle into your length; occupy as much of your length as you can. Then feel out to the edges of your skin. Feel out beyond your body, to the right and left, and extend your energy out into the field surrounding you.

2. Now settle some more. Look into that open view and let yourself feel where you're headed in your life, feeling into what is possible for you, what you desire.

3. Now feel into your back. Survey from the top of your head all the way down to your heels, asking what you notice when you feel into the back side of your body. Can you feel behind you? What is your experience of what is back there? Would you name it dark or light or something else altogether? Let yourself feel as much as you can what is at your back—your personal history, the support you've felt from others in your life, the years of your lived experience.

4. As much as you can, stand solid in yourself, your dignity and worth, the ways in which you've built relationships and felt love, and let yourself feel the dark and the light as an integral part of who you are here, now. Facing forward, centered and grounded, name one slice of darkness that you are now willing to accept as part of who you are. Speak out loud what you now accept.

20

The Doorway of the Gap

*O*n the London underground there's a sign that any writer has to love: *mind the gap*. As you approach the platform to wait for the oncoming train to stop so that you can board it, you can contemplate the admonition. Yes, this is a physical gap that exists between platform and train, but you could just as readily imagine all sorts of possible gaps that need to be navigated to move forth.

A gap tends to have an accompanying physical sensation. When boarding the underground train, there might be the sensation of slight vertigo as you step across the gap. You're probably not going to fall down into that gap, but something in you knows you might. With writing, the gap often exists as we begin a new piece, as we cross over that particular threshold. Or whenever we begin writing there is often the sense that our words aren't matching the depth of what we're feeling. The gap that we have to mind is the space in-between—we have a passionate inkling about what we want to say, but we can't find the words to match that passion.

When we're in the territory of the gap with our writing, we might feel that vertigo sensation in our guts. We might feel frustration at our language not meeting the quality of our emotion or what it is we are describing. The gap exists in that space between what is deep within you and how you make sense of that and bring it into the light. I once wrote a poem about getting thrown by my sensei on the aikido mats. I wrote about the "throb of the *yes* of the moment" when I was suddenly in the air, somewhere between pain and pleasure. At that time I wrote that I experienced a place of no-thought, where I got to feel the cleanliness of the energy coming from all of him and that I "knew what it meant to be at the rope's / middle, that still and centered point / between opposing forces tugging for position."[1]

What *is* the throb of the *yes* of the moment asking you for? What are you covering up? What is your rope's middle? What is the speech that might reveal you? How do you make the whole audience turn toward you with all your light?

It's often a matter of navigating that territory of in-between. What comes from deep within us that we are drawn to write about? What in the external world helps us to name this territory? As we mind the gap, we learn how to do both—to feel from the inside out and also from the outside in. We become that still and centered point from which our writing issues forth.

 ## *Practice This*
Finding the Rope's Middle

Here's a way to practice knowing what the gap might be between you and the subject or object of your writing. As you move through this practice, you'll learn how to close that gap and write from a new place. Begin with a brief centering practice, as follows.

1. Make yourself tall by expanding as much as you can through your spine and lifting yourself upward on the inhale, while your feet are still planted on the ground.
2. Take a long exhale down the front of your body as you soften from the inside out.
3. Fill the room you're in with your energy, letting it expand out from you in every direction.
4. Take another deep inhale and exhale as you look into the space all around you.
5. Now take up your pen and begin by listing quickly the objects in your space that are drawing you in. Choose a half-dozen objects.

Just list them—woven plate from Thailand, hand sanitizer spray, lotus candle, mug full of large paper clips . . .

6. After you list the objects, walk around your space and pick up each one, letting yourself feel the object as if for the first time. Pick it up, feel it, and then put it down. Do this until you've touched all your objects.

7. Now choose one. Or let it choose you. Bring that object to your writing desk and place it in front of you.

8. First answer this question: What do you notice right now about what the gap might be between you and your object? What is that gap made of? What does it make you feel?

9. If a physical sensation has arisen related to the gap—or anything else—then acknowledge the sensation and let it move through you. You can take deep breaths, or move around your space, or jump up and down, or shake your body loose of that sensation.

10. Now pick up your object. Hold it closely. Touch it, sniff it, press it against your cheek, do whatever makes you physically connect with your object.

11. As you hold your object close, maybe against your heart-space, close your eyes and ask yourself what within you wants to be expressed through this object. Tell the object what it reminds you of, what it makes you feel, how it informs you.

12. Place the object down on your desk and begin to write about it. Take ten minutes to do this. Look at the object, remember what it was like to feel the object, feel within yourself, and write at that confluence. Describe the object in a way that lets your readers know how that object has touched you, what it has touched, what difference it makes.

21

The Doorway of Hiding

Sometimes our greatest fears live right beside our greatest desires. This often shows up as we get closer and closer to speaking our truth. Sometimes our greatest desire is to be seen, to be visible, to be known, to have our words affect another. And that desire lives right up against a huge fear of being seen. This being at odds with ourselves can wreak havoc on our writing lives. We want to get words down on the page that will speak across difference and create a world that matters to someone else. But when we get close to doing just that, we suddenly feel exposed. Such a contest leaves us depleted and possibly unable to write a thing.

A writer I knew once spoke about her own difficulties of hiding out, which she described as a kind of holding back that made her camouflage herself, almost as if she were writing in the third person. Her biggest desire was to find her dramatic, passionate, personal voice rather than continue to keep herself away from that voice by not penetrating to the heart of what she wanted to say. Interestingly enough, for her it wasn't that she had a hard time writing; the act of writing actually came easily and readily. But when she wrote, she could sense the mask more than the blood and bones of language. She knew she had to get inside herself, to feel herself from deep within first, to know that her vulnerability and strength could coexist. Her strongest desire was to write from her heart and her gut.

At other junctures we might hide ourselves away and not speak the truth because we're afraid that the truth will hurt someone we care about. So rather than write or speak what we see, what we know, what the reality of our own experience tells us, we skirt around it, we sidestep, we turn away, we stay quiet, we clutter our language with too many words, we don't dig deep into the heart of what matters. This can show up as vague language, too, as skimming the surface, as writing about something else that doesn't matter to us as much.

We may express our hiding—our hesitation and apology—in the words we choose or the words we hesitate or refuse to use. Perhaps I feel a certain way but perhaps not. Maybe what I see is that my mother, father, brother, or ex was or is an alcoholic, and maybe I want to describe that state of being and its effect on another human being. But I'm concerned that this will hurt the others' feelings and maybe I won't do it because it's likely that they'll read between the lines and know I'm writing about them.

What are we really hiding from? *Discomfort. Exposure. Lack of safety. Repercussions. Being seen. Our own ignorance. Our own power. The truth. The lies. The validity of our own experience. Our own majesty.*

 ## Practice This
Facing What's Hidden

Once again we work with shining a light on a particular way of being—in this case, how we shape ourselves into hesitation, apology, or hiding out. As we identify what is hidden, face it, and extend our good energy toward it, we find courage.

1. What's a topic or idea that you've wanted to work with in your writing but that you've avoided or hidden yourself away from?
2. How do you hide? What is the shape of your hiding? Get into that shape, exaggerate it, and ask yourself if it has anything to tell you. How do you feel when you are hiding?
3. Now write the topic or idea down and place the piece of paper on the floor in front of you.
4. Stand over your topic or idea, read it aloud, and let yourself feel what happens when you face into this topic. What are you noticing?

Pay attention to where your energy moves in your body and mind, what the quality of that energy is, how you are in relationship to feeling the energy of this particular topic or idea.

5. You may be quite stirred up by experiencing your topic head-on. You may want to hide even more. Let yourself do that. Just realize how you do it.

6. Now come back to yourself standing over your topic on the piece of paper. Know that you can choose to engage with this topic, or you can choose not to. Up to you.

7. If you choose not to go on, then spend five minutes writing about what you saw, felt, and learned about your own hiding. Write down what you understand now about the relationship between the difficult topic or idea and how you can hide from it.

8. If you choose to go further, let yourself experience your topic more fully. Stand over it, feel the energy moving down through your legs and feet and into the earth. Imagine that the ground beneath you is a large field. Let yourself feel that ground, that largeness, as you also feel your topic or idea.

9. Extend your arms out in front of you, palms facing upward. Feel the energy softly moving through your arms and out your fingertips, out toward the horizon. Keep feeling grounded while you also extend your energy outward.

10. Put your topic or idea way out there on the horizon. Keep extending your energy through your arms toward that topic or idea. You might say out loud: *I am solidly here, standing on my ground, and extending my good energy toward [topic]*. Really let yourself have this time and space to feel the solid, huge ground beneath you, your body on that ground, and your desire extending out from you.

11. Now pick up your piece of paper, slowly sit down with pen in hand, and, from the knowing that you possess right now, write for ten minutes, facing into your topic with as much courage as you have right here, right now.

We have to find our way to a willingness to expose our true language, to hold ourselves with care as we do this, but to stop being so careful. As we strip away our tendencies to be careful about every little way we express ourselves, as we hone our language to be less hesitant and apologetic, we become more and more able to deliver language from a core place in ourselves, a daring place. We build our power from within; we trust that we can be more open and vulnerable, and within this is our deepest strength. If we can be fully with ourselves and willing to expose what is hidden deep within, our words will affect others. The blood will return to our voices.

22

The Doorway of Difficult Emotions

*T*hroughout the trajectory of our lives, we often find it necessary to hold in emotions that can't be expressed in a particular time and place or to particular others. Or at times we must ward off emotions from others that are either unwanted or unwarranted. It could be a matter of safety. It could be that we're afraid we'll hurt someone we care about. Or it could even be that we're afraid of the power of the emotion we think we might feel, so we hold it back.

Consider how you would accomplish this kind of holding in. Imagine that someone says something hurtful to you, and you feel yourself about to burst into tears, but you're in a meeting room with ten other coworkers, and you know this would not go over well. What do you actually do to not cry?

You probably found, as you considered the question, that to avoid crying you had to contract some part of your body or to turn away from what was going on with this hurtful person. Maybe you squeezed your eyes. Maybe you held your breath. Maybe your heart clenched, and you let it clench even more and harden a little so that you wouldn't cry. There are so many possible responses.

There are, of course, all sorts of emotions that we feel throughout our lives. Depending on the family we were raised by and the culture that chiefly informs us, some emotions are acceptable and some are not. We learn this very early on. And we learn ways around feeling the emotions that are not acceptable, for whatever reason. Our bodies are shaped by our particular emotional experience. Just as you learned to stifle tears, you've continually been navigating your emotional life through your body since you were quite small.

Emotional experiences and our accompanying bodily response and shaping occur over and over in our lives. The repetition lives in our bodies as a contraction and becomes part of our physical structure. If the response happens enough and takes hold in us over time, you can behave in a particular manner without even knowing you're doing it. This unconscious muscular holding becomes automatic and invisible to us and is called armoring. As you can imagine, armor is sometimes absolutely required; it's how it got there in the first place. But over time it can prevent us from feeling ourselves or from having choice around what we are able to express.

When we are unable to feel ourselves, we cannot feel into others or the world around us, which constrains our writing. The more we can soften the contracted places within us, the more fluid we become and the more able we are to let emotions run through us without attachment or blame. We can stop holding on to what's difficult to feel or be.

One client once said that she realized she veered away from her essential self when she found herself unable to let emotions run through her. She realized that she had to learn to stand with the energy of her emotions as they arose in her rather than resist them. If she could stay with the rising emotion and allow words to arise even from this difficult place, she found she could ground the energy of the emotion. Rather than be overwhelmed by it, she could follow the emotion and let it inform her. Rather than numbing herself to the rise and fall of a particular emotion, she began to feel herself more. This was a huge piece in trusting her own voice and spirit and cultivating the ground for her voice's development and rightful existence in her life and life's work.

Consider your own experience and let yourself search back through your history and review the times you've held in a powerful emotion rather than expressing it. Also consider times that you've warded off strong emotions from another. Perhaps they were screaming at you. Perhaps they loved you and you didn't love them back. Perhaps they laughed at you. Consider what you do when a strong emotion arises within you. Do you let it move through you, or is there a way that you stop it from arising? How do you stop it?

 ## *Practice This*
Letting Difficult Emotions Speak

Let's explore the ways in which we can express powerful and sometimes difficult emotions rather than holding them back.

1. What came up for you as you considered holding in powerful emotions arising within you or warding off powerful emotions from another? Free-write about this topic for at least five minutes. Describe how you hold emotions in. What is the shape your body takes as you do this? What do you feel or not feel as you do this?

2. What is an emotion that you have the most difficulty expressing? Write the emotion in your notebook.

3. Center yourself. Consider a time recently when this emotion began to rise in you. Let yourself feel the situation that caused the emotion. As much as you can, imagine yourself back in that situation. Rather than suppressing the emotion, invite it to appear again.

4. As you let the emotion in, what do you notice in your body, in your psyche, in your mood, in your energy?

5. If this is difficult for you, I'd invite you to two-step with the emotion. Place the difficult emotion in front of you and step-turn around it, with it, as if in a dance. See if this loosens anything up for you. What happened when you two-stepped with your emotion?

6. What could you do or be now that would let the emotion express itself through you? Try this: As you let yourself feel the emotion rising in you, make more room for it. Stand firmly but not rigidly on your ground, feeling your legs supporting you. Move strongly from your hips, let your arms swing like ropes at your side as your

hips swing first to the right, and then the left. You can vary the speed of this movement; your hips lead powerfully, and your arms swing to the right and left following your hips' movement.

7. Now stop and settle. Open your arms out to the side so you can feel your chest open. Ask: What does the emotion want to say? Take a few minutes to write down anything that occurs to you.

8. Now ask: What does it feel like to give this emotion full range? Write for five minutes, letting the emotion speak through you. What does it know? What has been revealed to you?

23
The Doorway of Disorder

*D*id you ever look around your writing space at all the papers strewn there and wonder how you get anything done at all? Or are you neat, putting away each piece of paper when you're done for the day? We all have different ways of getting our work done. I know a writer whose space is always pristine, whose books are neatly on their shelves in alphabetical order by author, whose desk is clear, whose work is organized precisely in file drawers, and who writes gorgeous, impeccable poems. Maybe disorder exists for him in the secret chambers of his psyche or even at his desk when he's alone. Or maybe not. I worked with another writer once who quoted to me something she attributed to Miles Davis: "Jazz is a musical form constructed out of disorderly impulses." She was feeling that she needed to find her own disorderly impulses in the process of her writing to be able to get to what was essential. For her, this became the necessity of disorder.

Sometimes we can create a cycle, too, of order and disorder. We find our own way through order and disorder as we write and move in our space, create and re-create, and move deeper and deeper into finding our own process.

You might spend hours pulling out journals, working in them, moving from those pages to another notebook that you use for new work. And then a thought arises that sends you to your bookshelf, searching for that author you once knew who wrote something directly related to what you're attempting to say, and you want to read that, right now. By day's end, what is strewn about is a record of your thinking and moving through that day's writing process. Maybe you end the day by putting away all that you have unearthed. Part of the beginning cycle for the next day might be that you need surfaces to be clear so that you can begin again.

Sometimes you can get caught in this cycle of order and disorder and have some self-judgment around what's right and not so right. You may want things to be neat and attempt to impose an order and schedule that you use in other areas of your life. Writing requires a fair amount of not knowing what might occur, not knowing exactly where you're headed. This isn't necessarily comfortable, especially when you realize that the messiness might extend into your inner life. The creative process is both raw and messy by nature. The territory you occupy when deep in such a process is anything but black and white.

Maybe you even feel drawn into this potential new way of being, one in which you are able to let go of preconceived notions about anything, dive into unknown territory, and play. I recall a client who spoke of the polarity of creativity on the one hand and productivity on the other. She identified rigidity in herself when she was in what she called production mode. She produced, she said, to fit in, to belong. In this place of producing she left herself behind, didn't trust herself, never felt that she was good enough. But as she figured out how to be present and to listen to herself, she found that she believed that she added value by giving to others creatively, in the moment. When she thought about what it meant to be creative, she knew what she needed was to find a place of her own making that could encircle her as she wrote. She needed to create a field to step into to allow her expression to take root. For her the qualities of such an unstructured place included joy, animation, lots of color, messiness, and vibrancy. She named her place the creativity house.

Disorder can bring you right to the edge of your vulnerability. Being vulnerable is where the juice is, even if it scares you. Surrendering to what's beyond your conscious mind and entering a place of both play and struggle helps you to embrace the raw, vulnerable, messy nature of true self-expression. You leave your critics at the door, cross the threshold, and connect widely and deeply.

 ## *Practice This*

Instigating Messiness in Your Own Creativity House

Try the following steps as a means into a more playful approach to your creativity—a way to bring messiness into your process for the sake of more vibrancy in your writing.

1. First, dig up a piece of your writing that feels incomplete or unsatisfying to you and place it on your writing desk.

2. Be sure you will be uninterrupted for the next ten minutes. Then read through steps 3, 4, and 5 before you begin your sitting practice. Settle yourself into a comfortable seated position. Then set a timer for ten minutes and begin steps 3, 4, and 5.

3. Letting your breath be deep, with an inhale and exhale of the same length of three seconds, follow your breath as it fills your lungs and belly, and then is released out of you on the exhale.

4. As you are settling into your breath, let yourself imagine you are entering into a kind of adult playpen, a bordered space that you can fill with a mess of your own making. What objects would you place in your space that would feature color, animation, and vibrancy? As you surround yourself with these objects, let each one encompass you in its vibrant, colorful, alive field.

5. You can fill the space as much as you want. There can be disorder. You may find that one object pulls you in more than another, one sensation more than another. Just notice what happens as you engage with each object in your playpen.

6. As you come back from your journey inward and open your eyes, move slowly to that piece of writing that feels incomplete to you. It may be that you didn't get down into the subject in satisfying ways. It may be that the piece feels too wooden. Maybe your writing skims the surface, and you want to dig down into its next layers beneath that surface.

7. Stand and read your piece aloud. Encircle yourself with your imaginary playpen of vibrancy, color, and aliveness. Now ask yourself what it would take for you to be messy and raw with this piece of writing. Not to know the outcome of creating such a mess. What do you feel as you consider stepping into your own messiness and rawness? What arises in you in relationship to this piece of writing? Let yourself be in the playpen, tossing ideas around you.

8. Now take one idea that came to you in furthering your piece of writing by creating a mess and stirring your pot of uncooked raw material. Follow that idea. Maybe it is sending you to another piece of writing of your own or another's. Pull that piece of writing or book out and put it in front of you. Maybe you suddenly wanted to draw. So draw. Maybe you want to move now. If so, move mindfully around your space, asking what's the biggest, most fun mess you can make to help you through.

9. Whatever arrived for you to create your mess, follow it. You could be feeling like your piece of writing is beside the point, and you're going into uncharted territory. Let yourself go there. Dig and explore, laugh and cry, follow and believe. When you've rolled around in your mess long enough (you'll know), stand apart from it.

10. Take three deep centering breaths as you gaze at the mess of your creativity. What do you notice now? How do you feel? What do you see?

11. Now take your piece of writing and incorporate what you discovered in your bout with messiness. Weave and bob with the writing you already completed, adding to it the color, vibrancy, and aliveness of your experiment with mess.

Part Four

The Roar of Your Writing

- ▶ See how to express centrality in your writing through image and emotion.

- ▶ Discover how directness adds power to your work—for yourself and your readers.

- ▶ Unearth the physicality of your own voice, its repertoire and emotional range.

- ▶ Explore what it means for you to gather your raw material, as well as yourself, as you dive into new writing.

- ▶ Define what roaring means to you and step onto your own roaring path, discovering concepts that help you persist.

- ▶ Learn about re-visioning and see how to hone your writing by feeling the words in and through your body, working toward more precision and energy.

- ▶ Experiment with delivering your work wholly and fully to an audience, a necessary step in your evolution as a writer.

24

Finding What's Central to Your Work

As creative writers, the source of our writing is ourselves. That may sound simple, but of course it's not. We have to find ways to craft language that meets the emotions that are making themselves known beneath the surface. As Chinese poet and critic Lu Chi says in *Wen Fu: The Art of Writing:* "It is like following a branch to find the trembling / leaves, like following a stream to find the spring."[1] And it's not just our emotional lives that want to be revealed through our writing; it's also our characters, our memories, our sensations, our urgencies, our ways of seeing the world and describing it, our obsessions, our commitments, our political viewpoints, and on and on.

But how do you really know and communicate what is central to you and your work? In an overarching way, finding the central core for your writing relates directly to much of the work we've been engaged in throughout the course of this book—feeling into and expressing what we care about, what we're committed to, what we stand in and for. What is central to our writing is what is central to our lives. What have you always been passionate about that wants to find expression now in your writing? Ask yourself what your most pressing questions or themes are. What issues do you want to delve into? What do you most care about expressing? You may already know the answers to some of these questions, or you may want to do a free-write in which you explore what those answers might be. Take the time to do that now.

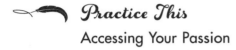

Practice This
Accessing Your Passion

Finding what you're passionate about can lead you into the central core of what is next for you in your writing.

1. Stand in your writing space, settle with three deep breaths, and center yourself by feeling your ground, your full height, the sky above you. Let the sunlight into your heart. Feel yourself rooted, but also how you can extend your energy all around yourself— front, back, right, left, above, below.

2. Now feel inside yourself; you might even place a hand on your heart and another on your belly. Breathe again into heart and belly.

3. Ask yourself: What have you always been passionate about that wants to find expression now in your writing?

4. Speak aloud your answers to this question, letting the words come forth in whatever manner they need to. Keep asking as you keep referencing your heart and your belly. Let your words echo in the room and also inside yourself. Jot down key points of what surfaces in your speech.

Once you have a sense of what is central to you and what it is you want to carry forth into your writing, you can begin to look at how centrality plays out in the writing itself. Consider that what is central to a piece of writing could be delivered through images, emotions, memories, dialogue, or the ways in which your characters interact with each other. Centrality could be expressed through a color, your choice of words, a mood, a particular time frame in history.

Imagine that one of your central themes, obsessions, concerns, or beliefs is that you can never really know another human being. Maybe this originated out of your personal history—you didn't know your birth father or mother, for instance. And then you acted this belief out throughout the course of your life and your relationships. You know many people intimately, actually, but this belief lives at your core. And now you want to put some flesh on the belief by writing a piece that faces into it. But how huge this topic is and how abstract!

Centrality asks us to be specific and consistent. To choose a lens through which to view the topic at hand and to use that lens relentlessly. To focus both on the overarching central core as well as on the ways in which you can describe that core concern through the use of particular images or emotions. It is quite tricky to find a way to do this in your writing. You may be wondering how you could possibly begin. It helps to take on an attitude of play and a willingness to come at the writing from several different angles. It's not really possible to know what we are going to say before we utter the words, but we can hold the intention of our central core concern alongside our intention of conveying that core in a concrete way.

One possibility for wanting to convey this core belief that you can never really know another human being is to create a dialogue about this between two characters. Through them, you reveal the intricacies of this belief, given who these characters are in your writing. Or you could brainstorm a bank of images that relate to this belief, such as a fog-ridden sky, the veil that the nun who taught your catechism class wore and how you could never see her face, a room full of gray paintings—whatever arises as you allow your memory and emotions full reign and funnel what arises into concrete images. What fun! The point, as always, is to make what you write utterly your own.

Practice This
Rowing with Your Passion

Use this practice to join your body with what you are most passionate about. The rowing practice is a great way to powerfully align yourself with your passion and to write from that alignment.

1. Take out your notebook and write down what came to you in the earlier practice when you delved into what most wants to find

expression in your writing now. What are you most passionate about expressing?

2. Let's begin by rowing with your passion. Place your left foot comfortably in front of your right and settle yourself in this standing posture. Letting your hips be the movement generator, begin to slide your hips forward and back as you inhale forward and exhale back.

3. Now add your arms to this movement. Gently lift them up parallel to the ground, palms downward, fingers curled under as if you have oars in your hands and you're rowing a boat. As your hips move forward, your arms also move forward on the inhale. As you exhale, bring both your hips and your arms back, letting your hands stop at about level with your hip bones.

This represents the entire rowing movement. The figure to the left shows the hips sliding forward as the arms move forward, as if rowing. The figure to the right shows the hips and arms moving back to complete one cycle of rowing.

4. Do the movement six times with your left foot forward, then switch your feet so that your right foot is forward. Now do the rowing movement again from the other side, remembering to move from your hips and let your arms follow. Your hips generate the power in this movement while your arms generate a gentle flow from that power.

5. Once the movement feels more natural to you, then approach it again with your left foot forward. This time as you row, bring in what you are passionate about expressing in your writing. As you breath in and out and generate power and flow from your hips and your arms, let this passion surround you, inside and out.

6. Switch your feet again and row with your passion from the other side.

7. When you have completed this practice, place your feet parallel to each other and stand facing an open space. Hold your hands on your belly center and let the passion settle there, deep within.

8. Now take up the pen and begin to write about rowing with your passion. Try any of these approaches. Write about your passion by beginning each line with "Now, I see . . ." Or with "I wish . . ." Or you might choose someone to write to about your passion in the form of a brief letter: "Dear Michael . . ." Or even begin each line with someone's name whom you want to write to: "Amelia, I want to say the veil has fallen off . . ." And so forth. Allow your memory and emotions to surface and be as concrete as you can, giving what you see and feel a specific face and spirit. As you write, remember the feeling in your body of moving from center as you rowed with your passion. Let yourself feel into the power you generated in that movement now, as you write.

25
Becoming Direct

*I*f somatic work gives you access to the full energy of your being, as a client once told me, then your practices help to place you right into that embodied, energetic sense of yourself. This might be a new way of being and seeing for you. Of course, as you gain more and more access to these energetic aspects of yourself, doors keep opening as you stride deeper and deeper into not only new understanding but also new worlds—and words.

The wild and wonderful thing about somatic work is that it continually reveals yourself to yourself. If you go at it wholeheartedly and sincerely, with open heart and mind, you will see aspects of yourself you haven't witnessed before. What's exciting about this is that you can begin again and then again to know yourself in differing situations, to understand your responses, to make new choices, and to acquire the boldness required to take new action in your life and work. Of course, this includes your writing. How could it not? As you feel yourself anew and see yourself anew in relationship to others, you necessarily increase your capacity for empathy, for being able to get out of your own way and see freshly, without any prior agenda getting in the way.

But seeing directly and being direct—no veils, no fog, no hiding, no fear, no collapsing—is itself a practice. Just as we move through our days centering, then recentering when we get off-kilter, being direct isn't a continual way of being. We have to nurture directness, practice it consciously, and learn from it as we practice to be able to access it when we need it. As we become more able to feel the old tugs, but also more able to gather ourselves in the present moment and feel into ourselves more deeply, we can have a new response. We can dare to be more direct from this place of knowing.

Directness can be a scary posture—one that might evoke haziness or indirectness as a strategy to avoid being seen or heard from, being disagreed with, or maybe being misunderstood. There are plenty of reasons to turn away from being direct in our writing, but it's where our power lives. Powerful writing comes out of the ability to face into, see, and communicate what might readily be ignored by others. Or as war correspondent Martha Gellhorn wrote in a letter to Hortense Flexner, her teacher and friend, in 1940: "If you see something, you write it, to give the exact emotion to someone who did not see it."[1] Building on your capacity to be direct in your writing helps you to put forth that "exact emotion."

I once worked with a client specifically on being more direct in her writing. It frustrated her that she never felt she got to the truth, her specific truth, when she wrote. The work we did was with the jo. At first, she felt awkward in the practice and didn't see how it could help her writing. The jo is, of course, very unfamiliar to most people, so it is often difficult to move with it. When you hold the jo in front of you, you immediately expand your field of influence. It is palpable. When you lift the jo overhead, and then bring it down in front of you in the form of a strike, you are strongly extending your energy out and downward with your breath and your spirit. There is no avoiding that this is a statement. Also when you bring the jo overhead and behind you as you hold it with both hands, you are creating a huge amount of openness in your chest, your heart. All of this can be a powerful metaphor and teach us about our discomfort, which in turn shows us what is ours to develop.

When she first wielded the jo, my client began by striking off to the side, which is very common. What became evident is the ways in which this off-to-the-side stance, which I'd venture to say showed up in her life as well as her writing, prevented her from transmitting her deepest truths. And this is exactly what she was committed to transmitting. Through being willing to be awkward and then to find her way, to shift her stance and herself enough so that she could make direct overhead strikes, she began to sense the relevancy in the practice. This new shape she was practicing—the open heart, open chest, open belly—helped her to receive, allow, and transmit a direct strike. After practicing for a while, she sensed how the practice opened her. She noted the difference in striking directly over her head rather than over her shoulder, saying: "It's invigorating, like I had to use all of myself, like I could be strong." And this newfound strength in using all of herself did translate to her writing—she began to surrender to the energy and pulse of her own truth. This developed into an honesty in her new work that was palpable. As she stretched into more of herself, I noted how the work touched me differently, too. Not only did she know she was being more honest and more direct, but I remember her reading me one of her new pieces and saying, with surprise: "When I read this to you, I feel my whole self behind the poem." Becoming direct by practicing being direct gives us access to that full energy, that whole self. As Ted Hughes once said about Sylvia Plath's book *Ariel*: "A real self, as we know, is a rare thing. The direct speech of a real self is rarer still. When a real self finds language, and manages to speak, it is surely a dazzling event."[2]

 ## *Practice This*
Finding Directness

There are several ways into finding your own manner of directness. In the last chapter you worked with what you are passionate about expressing in your writing and tried several ways into some new writing. Perhaps this challenged you in ways you didn't expect. Or maybe you have a piece of writing that has been difficult to write, or you've found yourself unable to clearly and vividly express yourself within this piece. Or you could ask yourself: What's an area or subject matter that I keep veering away from? Consider the possible ways that you have avoided being direct in your writing. Once you have found a subject or piece of writing that you feel could benefit from this lens of directness, then begin with these steps.

1. First reacquaint yourself with the piece of writing by reading it aloud in your writing space. If it's a subject that you're holding, then spend a few minutes considering what it is about this subject that you find challenging. Consider your own indirectness, how it keeps showing itself in your writing or in your consideration of a challenging subject. When you read your piece aloud or consider this difficult subject, notice what happens inside yourself—your sensations and mood or the shape your body takes or wants to take.

2. Now leave your writing or subject at your desk. Find an object that can serve as your wooden staff or jo. It could be an actual jo, a dowel, a broom, a walking stick, or poles—anything that is about three feet long that you can hold in your hands, lift overhead, strike with, and move with.

3. Unless you have very high ceilings in your space, you might want to go outdoors with your jo. Stand in an open space with about four feet of space in every direction out from your body.

4. First settle yourself with several deep breaths, grounding yourself on the earth more and more with each exhale. Now place your right foot comfortably in front of your left and settle some more. Bring in the memory of your piece of writing or your subject to the field around and in you now.

5. Hold your jo out in front of you, with your left hand at the base of the jo and your right hand about six inches forward of your left. The base of the jo should be resting at your center. If you move your hips around in a circular motion, the jo should follow that centered movement. This is good to remember: your center leads the way as your arms follow.

6. Just to get used to the movement, practice lifting the jo up and completely behind your back. Lift straight up the centerline of the front of your body and let the jo drop down the back side of your body until it is parallel with your body. The tip of the jo will be

This shows the starting position for holding the jo at your center with your left hand at the base of the jo and the right hand at a comfortable position, about six inches forward of the left.

Far left: This shows a front view of a figure lifting the jo completely behind, with the tip of the jo facing the ground behind.

Left: This shows the side view of the figure lifting the jo completely behind the body.

facing the ground now. In this posture, your elbows open outward as the jo moves behind you and your chest opens.

7. Once the jo is completely behind you, next slide your right foot forward as you bring the jo back over your head, and then downward in front of you in a striking action. Remember to keep your elbows bent a bit rather than locking them—you want to feel fluidity throughout your arms. The jo strike should stop at waist level. The jo will now be parallel to the ground when you finish your strike.

8. Try this overhead strike at least six times in a row. Bring the jo behind you on an inhale, and then slide forward and strike the jo downward as you exhale. As you strike downward, be sure to drop your hips, which provides the powerful downward striking motion. Let your arms be as relaxed as possible, and remember to hold the jo with both hands as you strike. Always let the motion originate from your center and be completed from your center.

This figure shows the final position once the jo strike has been completed.

9. Once you feel you can execute the general striking movement with relative ease, stop and settle yourself. Now bring to mind the piece of writing or the subject that was causing you difficulty. Remember what challenged you about the writing or the subject. Let yourself feel this again and notice any shift you sense in your body shaping or mood or emotional state. Now bring in the intention that what you really want is to be direct about this subject or piece of writing. You don't need to think about what this might mean; just let yourself feel your commitment to directness.

10. Now holding your subject or writing in the space with you, stand again with your jo, readying yourself to do several strikes. Speak aloud what it is you want to be direct about. Bring it right into the space surrounding you. Again, place your right foot in front of your left, holding your jo in front of you. Now execute ten overhead strikes. Take it slowly. After each strike, recenter yourself and recommit to directness around your writing or particular subject. Then strike again. After each strike, also notice how you feel. Are you connected to your commitment? What might you need to do to deepen your ground? Are you able to bring the jo clearly behind you? What does it feel like to have your chest so open? What is it like for you to strike so directly?

11. When you complete the ten strikes, bow to your jo and put it gently away. Then take up your pen and write for at least ten minutes. You can consider what you noticed about being direct with your body. Then write about your challenging topic or rewrite the challenging piece, bringing all your newfound directness to your words.

26

The Power of
Your Distinct Voice

*E*ach of our voices matters. Of course.

But what is *voice*? Webster's defines voice as "a sound produced by the body; the power or ability to produce such sound; an instrument or medium of expression (voice of the workers); a wish, choice, or opinion openly expressed; the right of expression; influential power; without dissent (with one voice)." Voice has both physicality and influence contained in it. It is derived from and is an instrument of the body. Our right is to claim that voice powerfully.

How do we know and feel what our rightful voice is? If voice is a physicality moving through our bodies, it makes sense that for the voice to move through us powerfully we need to be clear vessels. When our voice arises strongly from deep within us and finds expression through language and our fullest being, it's like a good, strong, necessary storm. We experience both relief and blossoming. When we are able to let our voice move through us unimpeded, others hear us, too. What becomes possible then is dialogue, exchange, and a certain depth of relationship, communication, and spirited commitment—and good writing, too.

Recently, when digging in some files and old music, I came across some cassette tapes from nearly four decades ago. Given that they represented a long-ago love affair and were potentially explosive, I decided to listen to them. One side contained my voice and side to the story; the other contained my lover's. Oddly, it was not the content that set my emotional state on edge but the nature of my voice—I almost didn't recognize it as my own. I'd been living in London for two years at the time, so my voice held a slight British accent, especially in the vowels. But it was much more than that. I heard a much softer version of myself. The pitch of my voice was much higher. I sensed appeasement in it. I would say that my voice was not connecting to my deeply felt emotions at the time—although I was speaking of grief, my voice did not meet the depth of that emotion.

This all puts me in the question now of the inner source of our power and how that relates to being able to express ourselves outwardly and to the way our voice moves through our bodies and outward into the air. I'm not judging that earlier voice to be less than, just noticing how unformed and different it was from the voice I am today—which hopefully represents decades' worth of growth! There's a deepening resonance in my voice now.

Language moves through our bodies in the shape of our voice; language is a sensation of sound. As we speak, we can take note of where that sound originates and how it moves through us. If you listen to the sound of your own voice, what do you hear? If you notice how words move through your body and form speech, what do you see or feel about that movement? If your body is an instrument or a vessel, there is a way that your voice is interacting with all of who you are as it makes its way through your body—history, mood, shape, anxieties, emotions, commitments, spirit.

Just as there's a repertoire of emotions available to us that we may not make use of, or know utterly, there's a range in our voices that is available to us to explore. It's a matter of coming to know the sound of our own voice so that we can make the choice to expand that range, if we want. We can allow more and more to come through our voices as we let more and more emotions express themselves through us. Just as we often have to open the door to what is next for our writing, we can open the door to the voice that wants to move through us. How we increase our ability to amplify our voice, to speak our complex emotional life, to connect our language viscerally through the voice of our bodies is, of course, a process.

Once we know the sound of our own voice, its tone, range, and timbre, we can get better and better at using our physical voice to help us write and rewrite. Just as singing aloud in our cars to no audience at all can help us free our voices, so can reading our work aloud in our writing space. We can listen for the origination of the physical sound. Where in our bodies does our voice derive from? What if we asked it to come from somewhere else? What would that be like? What might that allow or change in our writing? The more we inquire and feel into our voices, the more we begin to connect viscerally with what we must say, and the more our distinct voices will ripple out and find the shore.

 ## Practice This
Connecting Voice and Emotions

Working with understanding the range and expression of our physical voice and practicing our way to expanding that voice can help us dig deeper into the emotional content of our writing.

1. Select a piece of writing, your own or another's, that you love for its complexity and the wide range of emotions expressed within it.

2. Read the piece aloud slowly, making it your own with your voice, whether it's your writing or not.

3. Ask yourself these questions and write down your answers in your notebook:

   • As I read this piece aloud, where is my voice coming from?

   • What do I notice about pace, timbre, tone, or texture of my voice?

   • What is my emotional state as I read this and hear my voice behind the words?

   • Does my voice give life to this piece, or is there more range I could acquire to have my voice resonate deeply with the words?

Practice This

Expanding Your Voice's Range with a Kiai

We often don't get a chance to let our voices out, unfettered. The *kiai* or soul shout of aikido practice is a great way to expand your voice's expression.

1. Stand with your right foot in front of your left. On the inhale, raise your right arm up through the centerline of your body and above your head, with your little finger facing upward. Hold your left hand in front of your belly, hand perpendicular to the floor, little finger facing downward.

2. On the exhale, bring your right hand sharply downward as you slide forward. As you make this downward cut with your right hand, let the motion stop just above waist level. Try this a few times.

3. Now put the movement together: inhale and raise your right arm up, exhale as you slide forward and cut downward with the right hand as described above.

The figure on the left shows the beginning of the sword strike with the right arm raised. The figure on the right shows the movement of the downward strike, while shouting the kiai.

4. Now do the whole movement again and, rather than exhale, let
   out a shout from deep in your belly as your right hand comes
   downward. You can shout *ha, hai* (the Japanese word for yes, pro-
   nounced "high"), *no*, or *yes* as you move forward and strike with
   your hand sword.

 ### *Practice This*
Connecting Voice to the Writing

You've explored your physical voice's range in expressing complex
emotions as well as practiced expanding your voice through a kiai. As
you let yourself tap into that feeling of expansion as well as the sensation of settling, this practice will help you experience the effects of
both on your voice.

1. After practicing your kiai several times, let yourself settle. Stand
   with your feet hip-distance apart and parallel and just circle your
   hips first in a clockwise direction, and then counterclockwise. Let
   your breath settle itself deep in your belly as you circle.

2. Now pick up the piece of writing you chose earlier for its emotional complexity. Read it aloud again, this time letting yourself be
   informed by the kiai practice as well as the settling. Bring both the
   expansiveness of the kiai and the deepening of the settling practices to your voice.

3. Write about what you see and feel in your voice now. What
   has opened up in that voice? What is now allowed that was not
   before? If you don't notice a difference, write about that. What
   do you want for your voice's development in relationship to your
   body and to your writing? What's one new practice you can take
   up to help you get there?

27
Gathering

*W*riting requires us to gather. Gathering is multifaceted. We gather ourselves. We gather our raw material. We gather our disparate ideas. We might gather with others to write together or to read our work aloud and receive feedback. We each have to find trustworthy ways of working that consist of many sorts of gatherings.

Most days I don't just sit down at the writing desk and write. I gather myself as I clear the vessel through which words arrive. This happens through a variety of practices that include a sitting practice, a martial arts practice, a yoga routine. All these practices gather me and help to bring my energy alive in a way that's gathered, too.

Practice This
Gathering to Write

To take on body-centered writing you, too, can find your way to an array of practices that gather you so that you can come from your best writer-self as you begin. You have to find what fits for your own writing life based on where you are in your development, as a writer as well as what you choose to develop in yourself.

1. Here are some possibilities to consider for coming up with a set of your own body-centered writing practices to gather yourself before writing. Mix and match and experiment as you begin your

writing days. Choose two practices to commit to doing daily for the next two weeks. Experiment with using these practices to gather yourself before you write.

- Bow as you enter your writing dojo.
- Practice rowing at least six times per side (see chapter 24).
- Make hip circles and figure eights.
- Choose a centering practice from the book to engage with before you begin writing (see chapters 2 and 5).
- Sit for at least fifteen minutes, attending to your breath, letting your thinking self rest.
- Go outside with your wooden staff and do ten overhead strikes after speaking aloud what you are currently committed to for the day's writing (see chapter 25).
- Walk in your writing space in a mindful, centered manner, letting yourself feel the space inside you and all around you.
- Do a yoga routine.
- Two-step until you feel yourself unified within and able to reference the space around you (see chapter 6).
- Consciously choose your writing stance for the day's work: sit at your desk and see how this feels and then stand and assess that. Pick your seated or standing posture for the day's writing based on what you notice in each stance.

2. Keep a daily journal on what you notice as you bring gathering into your writing dojo: these can be brief observations. When the two weeks are completed, write about your relationship to gathering now.

The other sort of gathering is related to the writing process itself. One possibility is to capture words, phrases, lines, stories, images—all of it—in notebooks. As you gather all that touches you over time and begin to fill notebooks, you are developing a great source for further writing. Notebooks can be mined for the odd or inspired image, the riff that can turn into a poetic line, the dream that can lead to the start of a piece, the disturbance that still shakes you that you must uncover further. Keep journals when you travel: they often provide source material. Carry a notebook with you during the day and write down anything that strikes you sideways and asks to be recorded. Draw in your notebook, even if you don't know how. All these methods provide gatherings.

Once you fill a notebook, you can then spend time going through the notebook and seeing, sensing, and feeling into phrases or sections that hold strong energy in them. You could then type up these words, phrases, or paragraphs from the notebook and keep them in a binder that you can refer to later during a writing session. When you write, pick up what you've gathered and begin to settle yourself beside it and then ask: How do I want to give these words shape today? Sometimes your daily practice will have opened you to the answer to that question. When you're gathered, something comes alive within you that wasn't there before. Sometimes what has emerged has an urgency to it that must be expressed through language. Other times there is nothing, or it feels that way. In these cases, spend time with your gathered words in your notebook. Without intending a thing, you can still gather from this state of receiving. As you flip through the pages of your notebook, listen and receive what might want to be heard. This kind of listening can lead you to a word or a phrase that you've already gathered, but that is now coming alive in the present moment.

Gathering and following. Following and gathering. Words go down on the page, and they themselves create a direction, conjure new meaning, move forth, word upon word. Gathered language builds into lines, into a kind of progression, something that begins to have its own life, its own way on the page. This is the dance: words form themselves; you form words; words like each other and want to hang out together; you like words and want to use them—and then more listening. There's a shape that wants to happen on the page. Gather yourself to see what that might be.

The body is intricately involved in this process of gathering. Sometimes as we practice, we find we can take the somatic learning directly to our writing desks. It might be that we discover what it feels like to change our perspective—through the two-step, say, or through our centering practice. We remember how very simple it can be to shift perspective. We see again that we actually have so much more agency than we let ourselves believe. We might see that we gather ourselves differently when we are seated versus when we are standing. We may discover that when our head is up, this makes a huge difference to the stories we tell ourselves, to what we have access to in a moment's notice, or to how we feel about our capacity and abilities. We may find a stance that gives us access to a more open, fuller, clearer, more powerful, and more grounded place in ourselves. We can learn and see this in and through our bodies as we practice. We can see that a gathered, confident, grounded place is here within us, and we can access it readily.

 *Practice This*
Gathering Writing

Challenge yourself now to see what a gathering process could look like for your writing.

1. Choose several pieces you've written as you've completed practices and writing suggestions throughout the book. Select at least four pieces that spark something in you, that excite you in some way, even if you're not clear why that is. The writing makes you curious, or in its presence you feel more alive.

2. Now choose your method of gathering. You might use a new notebook. Read through the writing you have selected, capture words, phrases, images, even paragraphs that move you, and record these in your new notebook. Or you could decide to type up the chosen writing as it is and begin to gather the writing in a binder. Or come up with your own process, whatever that is. What's important is to find a way to honor what you've written by gathering it with the intention of revisiting it and working with it later. Your notebook or binder becomes a repository to draw from, a place rich with your own gathered images, phrases, and ideas that can lead you forth into new, exciting work.

28
Exploring Your Roar

*W*riting is as much about developing a relationship with the *you* who is a writer as it is about finding myriad ways to approach your work and get the best words you can down on paper. As you write, you encounter layer upon layer of who you are and what you are capable of. As you've seen over and over through the practices you've tried in the course of this book, we all have personal histories and cultural shaping that can sometimes corner us and cause us to hold back something vital in our expression, even as our desire to communicate that vitality is also strong. By now you've experienced ways to face into your habitual patterns as a writer. You've likely learned how to break into new territory. You may have experienced this: to express yourself you have to get out of your own way, but without doing the self-work required to know who you are—to face into your history, foibles, tendencies, dreams, and desires—you cannot get out of your own way.

None of this work comes readily or easily. The courage and daring that is required can sometimes feel monumental, but with persistence the possibility of becoming a better writer increases exponentially. We change when we engage all of ourselves, and this certainly includes our bodies, which again and yet again offer us opportunities rich with untapped knowing.

The whole idea of roaring came directly out of work with one client who had begun to develop a relationship with her writing. She wanted that relationship to grow and deepen, and she also wanted to roar. That sense of holding back something vital, beside her desire for that something vital to be expressed through language, felt very real to her.

This is really what her roar was all about: to find a way, *her* way, to give voice to what was most powerfully calling—her own way of seeing. She wanted to know herself deeply enough to be able to step aside from that self and let the words roar through her. She once wisely said that at first roaring was about "standing up, being seen, being heard, making a difference," but that her definition of roaring evolved into also "knowing and accepting yourself so much that is it not you that roars but the words."

Roaring is the ability to feel confident and sense your competency. It's remembering your purpose, being direct, realizing you can ask for support rather than do it all yourself, knowing that you're enough, taking the time to really consider, think through, and finish what is important to you. When you roar you'll be heard, taken seriously, and noticed. Your voice will come from a deeply connected place. You'll experience authenticity—in voice, speech, writing, and action. You'll speak your truth unabashedly.

What does it mean to reach your fullest potential as a writer? What would it be like to trust yourself enough to keep delving, diving, and surfacing anew in relationship to the writing at hand? How would you continue to roar onto the page with a clear, compelling, engaging, playful, inspiring, powerful intelligence? You have to be present for the writing that wants to emerge, trust yourself enough to persist down the path of roaring, show up consistently to the page, have a space for writing, and develop good habits around the work—knowing that once you commit to your work, your work will find you. As we expand our capacity to feel ourselves, we generate powerful writing.

Roaring is multifaceted. Realizing this helps us to identify our own particular roar and to persist in uncovering our unique expression. Roaring can be the outright, daring, full-bloom cry. Roaring can be the feel of the swing when we're pumping our legs and accelerating, roaring ourselves to the top, but it's also the falling back, the retreat down to earth; both are required for the full roar. Roaring is giving ourselves utterly as much as seeing what wants to emerge from the quieter self. Roaring is sometimes whispering—and a whisper can be just as powerful as a shout.

Our strength as writers is sometimes hidden in the shadows, sometimes overflowing, sometimes found in our vulnerability. Roaring as a writer is an adventure, a discovery, a willingness, a new way to know who you are. Knowing the cyclical nature of your writing life is crucial, too—reflection, research, writing, re-visioning, more reflection, dips into fallow territory (renewal time), more writing. And then working despite yourself. Working with yourself. Letting the writing at hand be your partner.

Much of what we learn as we bring ourselves to our own roaring keeps living within us as we continue on with our writing lives. As we've said before, we begin with ourselves, with knowing and accepting our own histories, who we are when faced with conflict, how we strive and how we let go, what love is in the face of the violence surrounding us—all this we must come to know so that we can express our own voices, write our own knowing onto the face of this world. And then we have to forget ourselves. We have to know ourselves so well that we can let ourselves go and see what wants to rise—through our hearts and minds and bodies, through our own language that is unique.

But it's not as if we do all the work on ourselves and we're done. Instead, we engage in the path of knowing ourselves, and simultaneously, we sit down at our desks, take up our pens, and dive into language from our current state of knowing. What makes this exciting is that we will always be facing a new page, a new self. We are never who we were yesterday or even this morning. We stay on the path of seeing and polishing ourselves, *and* we stay on the path of being able to step aside and let the words shine through. This is really about giving ourselves, pouring ourselves out. Writing can be the path to our own knowing. If we are a vessel for language to pour itself through, the writing itself is also a vessel that holds our precious words.

Practice This
Stepping onto the Path of Your Own Roar

Giving voice to our vitality as writers, our own way of seeing, requires us to get out of our own way so words can roar through us. Here's a way for you to discover what your own roar is made of.

1. To step onto the path of your own roar, first notice where you are. Become as present as you can within yourself and the space around you. Settle and listen. You can do some of the earlier practices to settle yourself—with breath, center, and alignment of head, heart, and hara. Ask yourself what you need to feel more deeply grounded and rooted.

2. Once you feel ready and present, ask yourself what it's like to feel yourself in this fully settled state.

3. What do you notice as you begin to occupy yourself more deeply? Take note of how you got to this state and what it feels like to be here.

4. Write for at least five minutes, answering these questions about your roar:
   - How do you want to give voice to your own way of seeing?
   - What are the qualities of your roar that you want to come into now?
   - What do you need to step aside from to be able to let words roar through you?

5. Bring the kiai practice back in now. The kiai, or soul shout, is a great way to let yourself feel your own roar. Pay particular attention to the nature of your kiai today. What is it telling you about the quality of your roar?

Kiai practice reminder: Stand with your right foot in front of your left. On the inhale, raise your right arm up through the centerline of the front of your body and above your head, the little finger of your hand facing upward. Slide forward with your right foot and on the exhale, bring your hand sharply downward. Try this a few times.

Then rather than an exhale, let out a shout from deep in your belly as your hand comes downward. You can shout *ha, hai, no,* or *yes* as you move forward and strike with your hand sword.

6. After you practice your kiai several times, ask yourself this: What's my roar made of? Do several more kiais as you hold this question.

7. Write for ten minutes, returning to the question of the nature of your roar, over and over. Is it gentle, forced, spirited, or daring? Does it come from your quiet center or is it made of your desire to give yourself fully? Let yourself discover what your soul is shouting.

29

Honing What's True: The Act of Re-visioning

*R*e-visioning is a separate task from writing. Never mix the two—that is, when you write, write unfettered. When you re-vision, your task is to make your original writing truer. To be a good editor of your own work, it is necessary to understand your own pitfalls as well as to know your strengths. To reach a depth of understanding in both, you have to write a whole lot. Write copiously and take chances in your writing. Experiment with new approaches, ideas, shapes, and voices. Write in as free a manner as possible, without allowing any voices in you or outside you to stop you. Realize that you are free to write in this wild manner because you know that you can revisit your work and revise it later. Remember that writing is discovery, and you will not often know what will emerge until you are in the process of writing and following where the words take you.

When you revise, be careful not to take the life out of your writing. Revising is really about re-visioning, seeing your language in a new way with a clarity that wasn't available to you in the first draft. To revisit your writing with fresh eyes, give the writing some time to sit before you begin to rework it. You'll have to find the right balance between being precise with language and keeping the original emotion and intent intact. You sometimes have to toss out words, lines, and even paragraphs that are dear to you to allow the writing's strength to come through fully.

You can return to your writing with new eyes if you think of yourself as an observer of your work. Fiction writer Robert Olen Butler says that a bad memory can serve you well when you go back into your own writing to revise it. In other words, the more you are able to forget yourself as the creator of a piece of writing, the more you will be able to go back into that writing as a reader-observer. Butler says this: "The primary and only necessary way of experiencing a work of literary art is not by 'understanding' it in analytical terms; it is by thrumming to the work of art. Like the string of a stringed instrument, you vibrate inside, a harmonic is set up. So to edit your work, you go back and thrum to it. And you go thrum, thrum, thrum, twang! And when you go to twang as a reader, you mark that passage. And you thrum on and twang on and thrum and twang and thrum and twang. Then you go back to the twangs and instead of looking at the twangy spots and analyzing them . . . instead of consciously and willfully applying what you understand with your mind about craft and techniques, you redream those passages. Rewriting is redreaming. Rewriting is redreaming till it all thrums."[1]

Allow yourself this reverie that Butler speaks of when you rewrite. A good part of what you will be looking for as you sense that thrumming is precision and energy. First, get a strong sense of what your precise meaning is, and then take away unnecessary words and refine others into the right words to energize your language. In the course of this stripping and replacing, you will inevitably be required to strip away something that you hold dear. Just because a particularly precious line or phrase doesn't serve your current purpose does not mean it will not serve you in the future. Save the precious bits you cut away; they may find a home in another piece of writing. Put these in your notebook or binder where you are gathering your bits and pieces of language to serve you in later writing sessions.

When revising, you also get to fix mistakes of grammar or usage. You can make your punctuation consistent throughout a piece. You can fine-tune your choice of words and get rid of repetition and clichés. You can ask yourself, over and over: Is this the right word, the right sound, the right image? Do the images work well together? Are your verb tenses consistent throughout? What is your writing yearning to be, and how do the words stop it from reaching that full potential? Is the tone of your writing supported by the words you've chosen?

Writers are often plagued with perfectionism. We're often busy trying to make everything right. This tendency is often fueled by an idea we've carried for a very long time about what "right" is. This idea we have of what's right is often no longer true. It might be something a teacher told us a long time ago that we've held tightly to ever since. Or right can have to do with not saying anything that would be outside a certain boundary we've created for ourselves, a boundary that might protect us from criticism.

If we are plagued with making it right, we lose the soul of the matter. It's like trying out a new recipe. We measure. We pay attention to the details that will lead to the success of the dish, such as proper amounts, the right temperature, and the method of mixing ingredients. But if we focus too much on these details, we forget to put feeling into our cooking. We forget to include ourselves—our love, our reasons for cooking a good meal in the first place, our desire to nurture. We forget the source of our making.

In the film *Like Water for Chocolate,* the young female character makes a cake while she is grieving, her tears mixing in with the batter. In a later scene everyone who takes a bite of that cake begins to cry. Sure, it's magical realism, but it's what we must learn to do when we're writing—to infuse our language with genuine care, with deep emotion, with all of our intelligence. The words then carry those emotions, which are felt by those who read our work.

We can certainly make it right when we edit what we write. But the first order of business is to make it our own. As we begin any creative project, really, what we need is to explore and discover. To find courage in the territory of not knowing. To find the central core of our care in language. And then to radiate out from that central core as we write.

It really helps to read your work aloud. You could read your work into a voice recorder, and then walk around the room listening to this voice that is now separate from you. You could also seek feedback from trusted listeners, and then listen to their feedback and make choices based on how that feedback reverberates within your particular sensibility. You have to listen inside yourself for what rings utterly true for you. When reading aloud, listen to where you stumble. Ask where the energy of the language decreases. Where do you (or your listeners) get bored? What's confusing? Ask yourself if what you're saying is what you really mean. Does the language work to accomplish your vision? Are the words you've chosen the best words to accomplish what you are saying?

Think of revising as a way of paying attention to and respecting your work. Your words on the page matter enough for you to give them focused attention and to rework them so they can shine. By writing and writing and writing, you will learn to hear what is best in your own work, and then keep what is best and edit out what is not. "The only purpose of revision is to get more deeply to the truth," says the poet Margaret Robison.[2] The purpose of revision, then, is to tell the truth of what has been experienced or imagined. Always stay with your own voice and vision in revising and in taking in suggestions from others about your work. As William Stafford writes: "revision brings a greater richness to the second time through and then the third time and so on. . . . For me, the language is never set like concrete; it's always like taffy. . . . The language changes, you change, the light changes."[3]

Re-visioning is a kind of remembering, and it helps to bring our whole body-mind to the process. By not only reading our work aloud but also feeling our work anew, we can re-vision our way to more powerful and truer writing. We can feel dissonance in our body. We know when the words we're using aren't the right ones because we feel that sense of something being unresolved or discordant. Learn to feel and recognize that dissonant twang in your own body and use it to inform you that something needs to change. Remember what dancing with a good partner feels like. When you're thrumming, you're moving your body in rhythm to another's, and you feel a sense of freedom and rightness and joy. When you're twanging, you get tripped up; you can't match your body to the beat, never mind to another's movement. Consider that you're dancing with language, and what you're aiming for is a kind of smooth gliding, a joyful encounter that has you feeling the meeting place between what's inside you and what matches that through your words on the page.

 *Practice This*

Thrumming to Your Own Beat

Choose a paragraph, stanza, or poem that has been challenging for you to rework and that you have some distance from. Follow these steps and see what happens.

1. Stand up. Take several deep breaths and feel your feet firmly planted. Let your chest be open, your head lifted. Let in the landscape that surrounds you.

2. Read your writing aloud, just letting it fill the space and you.

3. Sit down at your desk with your writing and a pen or pencil. Read it aloud again, slowly. This time take note of where the piece thrums and where it twangs. Mark the page with anything you notice. You might simply circle what twangs. Or use different colors to represent thrumming or twanging.

4. Slowly read aloud only what thrums. Let your words reach inside you. Let yourself smile. Return to what twangs and ask yourself any or all of these questions:
   • Are the words the right ones? If not, what words would be better in sound or sense? What's the best word for what you want to convey?
   • How does the energy of the language diminish? What can you do to amp it up?
   • Are you holding on to something you need to let go of? Let it go and see what opens up.
   • Have you unconsciously resorted to clichés? Eliminate them and replace them with original language.
   • Are you telling the truth? If not, find a way to what is forthright and dare to speak it now.

5. Re-vision your piece after answering these questions. Feel what you want to write, what you must write—bring the twangs to the level of thrums. You may need to get up from your seated position and do a two-step or several. As you two-step, hold the energy of your entire piece within you and in the space you are step-turning around. Then return to the re-visioning work.

6. Now stand again and read aloud your re-vision. I hope a smile is in order.

30

Tending the Fire

To continue on the path of your roar, you keep spiraling ever deeper into those hidden realms, while you also keep opening the door to the voice that wants to find its expression through you. What this will require of you beside persistence is huge amounts of forgiveness and compassion. You'll be asked, over and over, to believe that what you have to offer is of value and to offer it whether you yet fully believe that or not. Once you develop ways of consistently putting words down on a page, once you get used to opening the door day after day to what is there to be explored only by you, you will begin to have notebooks filling up with ideas and actual writing. You may find your way to a form that suits you—whether it's poems, stories, novels, articles, letters, or journal keeping, you will find your way. It's an ever-deepening process that asks again and again for your presence.

It might be that you struggle with following an idea, that initial exciting spark, to its fruition. It might be that when that initial idea becomes unwieldy, you give up rather than keep at it until there's a breakthrough. It may be that you're waiting for someone else to tell you you're a writer so you can keep writing. There are many possibilities, as we've all seen and experienced, for not continuing. A master is someone who stays on the path, who doesn't give up. There are many ways to stay the course.

But really you would not be here, you would not have read this far and done all these practices, if you weren't already on the path, with a huge desire to stay on it. You need to keep cultivating how to do that, how to continue to work with yourself so that you keep writing. How do you keep uncovering your excitement? How do you keep following your best impulses into new writing?

There's a concept in aikido called *zanshin,* which means continuing awareness, a continuation of energy, that prepares us for what is next. In aikido practice this shows itself especially in-between techniques. Executing a technique requires focus and attention from you, and once the technique is completed, maybe you let your attention stray or you even turn away. Zanshin would have you continue extending energy and presence toward your partner, toward the technique you thought you just completed. Rather than walk away or even slightly turn away, you continue that focused attention. In aikido terms you remain in contact with your partner, even though you are no longer touching her. Your energy is relaxed, strong, and stable, and because you are still fully *in* the technique, you are ready for whatever comes next, ready for the unexpected. Zanshin contains the present moment in it and also the future. Zanshin is continuity of aliveness.

The other concept from aikido that is closely linked with zanshin is extension. As we do a technique, we offer our energy to our partner; we extend ourselves energetically as we move. Where we place our attention, energy follows. As we practice we are building a body that is relaxed without slackness and extended without stiffness. As we extend our energy, we align with what or who we extend toward. What are you facing? What is the impact of your extending toward that? Extending is a deep listening—we extend into a situation to get a feel for it and we listen with our felt sense. As we extend, we influence.

 **Practice This**

Extending Attention toward an Object

Consider the ways in which practicing both extension and zanshin could affect your writing. As we learn to place attention on what we want to write about and extend our energy toward that subject, the subject opens up to us. Try this.

1. Put your right foot forward and bring your right arm up parallel to the ground, palm facing upward.

2. Relax your arm as much as you can as you begin to extend energy through that arm. Feel, sense, and imagine vital energy flowing through your arm and out your fingertips. Your hand and fingers are relaxed, too. Your hand is not rigidly held open, but rather curve your fingers a bit so that your hand has a slightly cupped shape to it.

3. As you continue to extend energy through your arm and hand, check to be sure your legs are solidly on the ground, and your knees are gently bent, not rigid. Let your breath come and go deeply as you keep extending.

4. Now with your arm still extended, walk up to an object or image in your writing space. Stand still in front of this and keep extending your energy toward it. As you extend and extend, keep relaxing your legs, deepening your breath, and extending toward the object or image.

5. Give this a minute or even two. As you extend, let the object or image enter you more and more. Keep increasing your listening, using all your senses.

6. Then when the minute or two is up, write what you learned about this object or image by extending toward it with all your attention.

Extension doesn't have effort in it. We extend from our center. We extend toward the things and people of this world so that we can increase our ability to listen to and affect others. Taking this into the writing realm, we can extend toward our subject matter, our characters, our sparks of ideas and keep extending as our pens move across the page. If extending is our listening, then zanshin is how we continue the listening—we don't turn away but keep focusing our energy, readying ourselves for the surprise around the corner waiting to be born through our words.

 *Practice This*

Continuing Awareness into What's Next

The concept of zanshin can help you to keep extending your energy toward a difficult topic, bringing more aliveness to your work. Consider what topic has been particularly hard for you to write about, something you've wanted to describe that keeps eluding you. Or maybe there's a spark of an idea that you haven't yet succeeded in following? Or maybe it's a person you've wanted to write about?

1. Choose a difficult topic and write it down in your notebook.
2. Center yourself in length, width, and depth, noticing the space around you. Feel into that space, expanding your energetic body to include it.
3. Now face north. Place your challenge as identified above in the space directly in front of you.
4. Take several deep breaths, then lift your right arm up and extend energy through your fingertips toward your challenge. If it feels right, walk toward your challenge with your arm extended. Take in whatever that challenge offers you.
5. Now face south. Continue the extension practice, as you face into your challenge and take in what it has to offer.
6. Now face east. Continue the practice, taking in what this view of your challenge has to offer.
7. Now face west. Continue extending toward your challenge, asking what it offers you from here.
8. Jot down any observations, feelings, sensations, descriptions that came to you as you did this practice. Within all that you noticed in this practice, what arose that you would like to follow? It might be a new realization about your challenge, a surprise turning, a furthering of some sort in relationship to your challenge. What is it? What would you like to deepen here?
9. Now stand with your feet hip-distance apart and raise both your arms up to waist height, parallel to the ground. Extend energy again through both arms now, with palms facing upward, elbows

slightly bent. Arms are relaxed but energy is moving through them. Begin to walk around your writing space, arms extended, energy moving through them. Vary your pace as you invite what you want to follow now about this challenge into the space with you. Keep extending. Keep moving. Keep feeling yourself in relationship to your challenge and what this furthering is.

10.   After a minute or two, stop and settle yourself, arms extending in front of you. Keep letting in what wants to be seen about your challenge and your deepening knowing of it.

11.   Sit down at your writing desk with pen and paper and write what you now know. How will you continue to practice zanshin in the face of your challenge?

31

Delivering Your Words

A natural progression that occurs as you keep writing is to want to share your work with an audience. This could come in the form of reading your work to one other person. It could be that you join a writing group and regularly read your work to others for their feedback. Eventually, you will likely find yourself in a public setting, reading your work to an audience of people you've never met.

What we must do as we read our work aloud is to make the writing on the page become an experience in and through our body as well as the bodies of our listeners. As language moves from deep within the writer, up and through her body, and out into the air, the writing can be felt and known. When we read our work with all of ourselves, we lift it into a three-dimensional space. We make the depth known.

The poet Robert Pinsky said that "the medium of poetry is the human body."[1] As we make contact with the words on the page with our voices, we dive back into what made us craft this piece of writing in the first place. We have to leave our egos at the door, trust in that original impulse, and step into that territory of openness and wonder from which those words originated. This isn't an easy task. It takes a certain emptying and willingness on our part as writers. The emptying is a kind of clearing of any emotional residue before we read. This can readily be accomplished by taking the time before you step onto that stage to center yourself, take several clearing breaths, maybe even sing or shout or *kiai* on your way to the reading—anything that serves to move what clings to you through and out of your system. Once cleared you are much more ready to encounter your writing anew and to deliver that encounter to your audience.

By strongly gathering our own energy we can meet our own vulnerability and deliver that as a strength as we read. When we deliver to an audience, we return to the original emotion that was the source of the writing. If we approach the words on the page freshly—even though they're quite known to us—we deliver those words to others afresh. Our voices have to find a match with the work at hand, and this will be different for each one of us as writers, as well as dependent on the venue and on the writing itself. What I mean by this is that every encounter we have with our own writing will have a different flavor to it, depending on many factors—the audience that evening, the friendliness of the space itself, whether we've done a good job choosing the work to read, how comfortable we feel in our clothes and our skin.

We all have different ways of preparing to read our work. It might help to have yourself organized ahead of time, to know the selection and order of the pieces you'll read, and to practice reading them over and over in your own writing space. Of course, you may be like a writer I once knew who brought his entire stack of hundreds of poems with him and selected on the fly, successfully. This takes enormous presence and practice and likely a willingness to show your disorganization proudly! For most of us, it helps to have a plan. It also helps to be willing to deviate from that plan as you read and as you feel out your audience. Keep making it new.

As you step onto the stage remember to take your center with you. By now you have a lot of practices to rely on—ones that would help you prepare ahead of time, such as the two-step before you go onstage, which will help you remember to center in transition, as you move into being onstage and being witnessed. You can always send more energy down through your legs, even place a hand on your hara, anything that helps you remember to come from deep within yourself as you read and to be as settled as you can be as you move from delivering one piece to the next. Take time to settle in-between pieces. Read slower than you think you need to. Choose someone in your audience who makes you feel good because of the way he or she is listening to you or looking at you and return to that person's countenance as ballast throughout your reading. Remember that your voice will find its way through your body and it will connect with the feeling and emotion of your words if you let it.

I recall hearing Ted Hughes read from his work in the early 1980s, in a very small library in an old manor house called Totleigh Barton, at the Arvon Foundation in Devon, England. He read as if encapsulated within each poem. The physicality of poetry became suddenly evident to me then, seeing this large man bent over his pages. The odd thing about his posture, this bending, was that in it he gained strength, and then gave that strength to his every word. His voice trembled, his words shook, and in all that expression of original intent and emotion, I trembled along with him. Something palpable grew and spread itself over us and through us that evening in Devon, something rarely seen or felt, something transformative. Because Hughes could so successfully return to the source of his poems, he could bring us there as well. He accomplished this by getting out of the way, literally bending his body to make space for the power of language to surge through him, and then over and through us. When we can step aside to this degree, we do become a vessel for language to move through us, and what happens seems to happen without us.

In the delivery our words are given air, literally, and they are witnessed. Again, this changes everything. We stand in ourselves, in our original intent for our piece of writing, in all the ways it has shaped us and we have shaped it—and we deliver. Something I've noticed in that delivery is that I hear differently. Maybe it's because I'm being witnessed. Maybe it's taking these words seriously enough to step forth with them and share them with an audience—the act of doing that—that shifts what I am able to hear. In this more attuned place, I can hear what I could not hear alone in my study, even if I read my work aloud there. In this witnessing, in this delivery, language takes on a new breadth.

We see more expansively when our work is witnessed and held by others. The edginess caused by being seen sharpens our senses. It's as if an entirely different force field is created when we have witnesses. Our words take shape in the air as they're released from our own consciousness. From here they enter the collective consciousness. With our words we share our energy and our insights, and the field between our consciousness and others' is widened, deepened. My friend Tom once said: "When words are given air, they vibrate and awaken connection, bring us together and move us, like ringing a bell once rung cannot be undone."

 ## Practice This
Embodying Writing from the Heart, Outward

One of the best ways to embody writing as you read it aloud is to memorize the lines. There's no page in front of you to hide behind at all, only your body and the words you are delivering. Even if it's not practical for you to memorize your work, or even desirous, try this practice as an experiment in the embodiment of language. Later, you will be able to use what you learn here as you read your work from the page. Or you might find you love having words within you at such an intimate reach, and you'll want to memorize even more.

1. Choose a short piece—a poem, a paragraph, or several lines of a longer piece. For the purposes of this practice, the piece doesn't have to be yours. Choose work that you resonate deeply with, whose emotional terrain you can readily enter into.

2. Go outdoors if that is feasible. Whether indoors or out, choose a spot, if possible, where you face an open horizon as you practice. Begin by settling yourself with breath, dropped attention, and a brief centering. When you feel settled within yourself, look at the words on the page, reading them first to yourself silently and letting yourself connect with what is being expressed, opening your heart to what you find there.

3. Then read the piece aloud, slowly. Read it several times aloud, trying on different tones of voice, differing volumes, following the emotion of the piece as you read. Breathe your way into each line, noticing what is required of your breath in each line. Let your-

self love the words, be curious, feel. Pay attention to how you are reacting to the words on the page from within. What about any sensations you are feeling? Listen as you read and attune yourself to the rhythm of the words, noticing any quickening that happens within you; attend to your natural bodily responses or any insights or increased understanding that you notice.

4. Once you feel a connection with the piece you've selected in this process of reading and repeating the words over and over and noticing your responses, take a brief walk about your yard or room, letting lines arise if they naturally do, but don't try to do anything. Just take a brief break from the reading.

5. When you return to your reading spot, just read the first line. Read the line several times, and as you read, again notice your relationship to the words and any changes you might be feeling as you open yourself more to the piece. After you have said the first line at least a dozen times, take another brief walk, repeating as much of the line as you remember without looking at the paper. Get into the sound of the line, the spaces between words, what you are feeling. Be even more curious about your relationship to the line now.

6. Of course, you may experience forgetfulness. Don't worry. Something will stick. Say those words. Then say what you think might be the next word, even if you're not sure. Bring some play into the process—remember no one is listening and you don't have to get it right. As you open to the piece, line by line, you will see how the places you can't remember are somehow calling to you to move beyond your current understanding. Keep at it, speaking and walking, until the line comes out of you readily.

7. Then take another short break, walking without agenda, letting the air and sky fill you.

8. Then add on the next line in much the same manner as the first one. You can start with just learning line two, but it can also help to speak line one and let line two naturally follow. Sometimes you gain some confidence as you speak the first line, which naturally delivers you right into the next line. Especially if it is your own piece, it is amazing to see how your body remembers writing the

work, and as you learn each line, you are piecing that memory back together—it is there inside you. This could also be true of a well-loved piece that you've known for a very long time but never taken fully to heart by memorizing it.

9. Work with this process until you have the entire piece committed to your heart and your memory. To do this you may need to spend several days with the piece. As you wake, say it out loud. As you go to sleep, say it again. Take a walk and say it again. Drive down the road, reciting.

10. When you have trouble remembering a line, take a few moments to consider what it is about that line that catches you. Ask yourself what you notice in your body as you come to that line, what it is that is making you lose connection. Read the line, noting how the words move you, or don't move you, and what the place of connection might be. Let your voice connect to that line in varying ways—shout the line, wail the line, cry the line, laugh the line—and see where your voice wants to land with those words. Then practice again, letting the line touch you as much as you can.

11. When you feel ready, recite your piece to another. This will feel different, no doubt. You may stumble; that's OK. Be gentle with yourself and begin again. Choose your audience wisely—let it be someone you trust deeply who supports your voice unabashedly!

12. Once your piece is part of you, and it will be as you go through this process, you have embodied the words and can call them forth whenever you want to. They live in you now. The piece has spoken deep inside you, and you have met the words with all of yourself.

13. Take a bow!

Claiming the Voice
You Have

Throughout the course of your engagement with this book, to whatever degree you dove into its ideas and practices, you have changed. Through stepping across the threshold of your own writing dojo, with your shoes removed so you can feel your own weight on the earth, you have learned what it means to enter new territory—within yourself and within your writing. Writing is risk taking. We step into this new territory and we find ourselves anew. It's not escape, but it *is* crossing a border. We all have to find our own way to create a life we can fully inhabit and channel into our work—a place we can give from utterly—unimpeded, a flowing stream. Our very own creativity house. Our very own dojo.

You've seen that we all have our unique challenges to find our way into that stream. We've explored those within these pages. Maybe through your work with the practices in this book you've found that you can deliver words from a core place in yourself; that as you increase your ability to find and return to your center, you come to know the spaciousness of *what is;* that you can keep a promise to yourself to show up over and over to the page; that you've found a way or two to expand into rather than contract away from; that you have more courage to turn and face what you had put aside and find healing there; that your fears are transforming from "a tsunami to a simmer," as a client once told me; that you've found ways to create doorways and cross thresholds that you didn't even know were possible. I wish all of this for you, and I know you can arrive at a place of freedom in your relationship with your writing.

As with any relationship, we have to nurture our writing lives day after day. We show up in our writing dojos with our practices close at hand and we work. Sometimes the work requires us to face ourselves in a new way before we can face the page again with as much honesty and daring as we can muster. Know that this work is ongoing, that there will be surges of excellent writing pouring out of you followed by a kind of fallowness that you will think you can't live with for another second. And then you'll wake up to another writing day, another realization, another sort of grappling with the task at hand. You will develop yourself as you grow as a writer.

Writing is a powerful force that helps us give form and shape to nothing less than our souls. From a place of relaxed power, language arises more honestly, more soulfully, more intentionally, more directly. This is a deeply integrated place where our true voices can shine and be heard.

It is my deepest wish that this book has helped you awaken and arrive at the page to give yourself utterly. Go forth with all your voices that are yours alone to deliver. Time to put your shoes back on, and do good in this world.

The Grace of Now

sometimes seasons change in a whirl of wind
then smoke into being.
sometimes we turn a corner
only to meet ourselves face-to-face.

if there's trembling to be had, have it,
if falling is the only way to touch the ground,
surrender to what's startling and right—

fierce light rising over dense mountain
the sound of water falling on stone,
and this body (always this body)
with its back of grief and front of desire.

what would it be like
to stay with yourself
(not ahead as if running for a bus
not behind as if left on the platform by departing train)
just here, just now
in this warm, still air,
earth moistened by yesterday's brief rain?

know that.
claim what is good.
then get up:
take your place in this world.

FROM GREGORIO, *ABYSS & BRIDGE*

Committing to Your Embodied Writing Life

*W*hat follows is a list of the practices included in *The Writer Who Inhabits Your Body,* section by section. My invitation is for you to choose at least two practices from each section that you will commit to making a part of your embodied writing life. Select practices that speak to where you are in your own development as a writer. You may find that some practices are suited as prewriting rituals, others work to move you through a writing struggle, and others work best for specific challenges that arise along the way. Once you find your patchwork of practices, work with doing your set of practices within the course of a week's time. Give the practices your full attention and spirit and change them up as you see fit. Most of all dive in, shake yourself up, and write from the fullness of who you are.

1. Center yourself, settle within, and ask yourself what it is you most want to develop in your writing or writing life. Spend some time feeling into this. Place your hand on your heart. Keep asking what's next for you, what is calling to you, where you're headed with your writing, what your dreams and desires are for that writing.

2. Refer to the list of practices that follows these steps. Look through the names of the practices in each section, noting in particular when you thrum to a practice—something's happening, follow it. Mark the practices in each section that call to you.

3. Take out your notebook and write down your first set of practice choices.

4. Decide when you would like to begin these practices and how practicing will fit into your day: which practices will you do before writing, which during, which after writing or later in the day as ballast or reminder to you to keep you on track with your writing life's development?

5. If it's helpful, you could now create a map of your first week of practice. Bring in these practices in a sustained way as part of your writing time. Have fun with this—draw or use color or dance or speak what you want your new writing life to consist of and how these practices can get you there. Know that you can always change what is not working for you.

6. Be full of rigor and compassion as you fill your writing dojo with the spirit of inquiry as you practice your way to mastery.

Part One: Center Is Everything

Part Two: Opening the Body to Language

Part Three: Turning Obstacles into Doorways

Part Four: The Roar of Your Writing

Notes

Preface. Words That Become You

1. Strozzi-Heckler, *The Leadership Dojo*, 98.
2. Rilke, *The Notebooks of Malte Laurids Brigge*, 20.

Chapter 3. Postures of Authenticity

1. Gendlin, *A Process Model*.

Chapter 9. Creating Space and Spaciousness

1. Lamott, *Bird by Bird*, 100.
2. Bachelard, *The Poetics of Space*, 184.

Chapter 10. The Writing Body's Emergence

1. Stafford, *Crossing Unmarked Snow*, 15.

Chapter 11. Writing, a Surrender

1. Harrison, *Saving Daylight*, from section X of the poem "Modern Times," 12.

Chapter 18. The Doorway of Fear

1. Carver, *Where Water Comes Together with Other Water*, 12.
2. Chödrön, *When Things Fall Apart*, 1.
3. Nin, *The Diary of Anaïs Nin, 1939–1944*, 125.

Chapter 19. The Doorway of Our Darkness

1. Lawrence, *Studies in Classic American Literature*, 15.

Chapter 20. The Doorway of the Gap

1. Gregorio, *The Storm That Tames Us,* 13.

Chapter 24. Finding What's Central to Your Work

1. Chi, *Wen Fu: The Art of Writing,* 12.

Chapter 25. Becoming Direct

1. Gellhorn, *Selected Letters of Martha Gellhorn,* 83.
2. Plath, *The Journals of Sylvia Plath,* xii.

Chapter 29. Honing What's True: The Act of Re-visioning

1. Butler, *From Where You Dream,* 37.
2. Schneider, *Writing Alone and with Others,* 113.
3. Stafford, *You Must Revise Your Life,* 60.

Chapter 31. Delivering Your Words

1. Pinsky, *The Sounds of Poetry,* 8.

Bibliography

Bachelard, Gaston. *The Poetics of Space.* Boston: Beacon Press, 1969.

Butler, Robert Olen. *From Where You Dream.* New York: Grove Press, 2005.

Carver, Raymond. *Where Water Comes Together with Other Water.* New York: Vintage Books, 1986.

Chi, Lu. *Wen Fu: The Art of Writing.* Translated by Sam Hamill. Portland, Ore.: Breitenbush Books, 1987.

Chödrön, Pema. *When Things Fall Apart: Heart Advice for Difficult Times.* Boston: Shambhala, 1997.

Gellhorn, Martha. *Selected Letters of Martha Gellhorn.* New York: Henry Holt, 2006.

Gendlin, Eugene T. *A Process Model.* Evanston, Ill.: Northwestern University Press, 2018.

Gregorio, Renée. *The Storm That Tames Us.* Albuquerque, N.M.: La Alameda Press, 1999.

———. *Abyss & Bridge.* Denver, Colo.: 3: A Taos Press, 2021.

Harrison, Jim. *Saving Daylight.* Port Townsend, Wash.: Copper Canyon Press, 2006.

Lamott, Anne. *Bird by Bird: Some Instructions on Writing and Life.* New York: Anchor Books, 1995.

Lawrence, D. H. *Studies in Classic American Literature.* New York: Penguin Classics, 1990.

Nin, Anaïs. *The Diary of Anaïs Nin, 1939–1944.* Edited and with a preface by Gunther Stuhlmann. San Diego: Harcourt Brace Jovanovich, 1969.

Pinsky, Robert. *The Sounds of Poetry.* New York: Farrar, Straus and Giroux, 1998.

Plath, Sylvia. *The Journals of Sylvia Plath*. Foreword by Ted Hughes. Edited by Ted Hughes and Frances McCullough. New York: Anchor Books, 1998.

Rilke, Rainer Maria. *The Notebooks of Malte Laurids Brigge*. Translated by Stephen Mitchell. New York: Vintage, 1983.

Schneider, Pat. *Writing Alone and with Others*. New York: Oxford University Press, 2003.

Stafford, William. *Crossing Unmarked Snow*. Ann Arbor, Mich.: University of Michigan Press, 1998.

———. *You Must Revise Your Life*. Ann Arbor, Mich.: University of Michigan Press, 1986.

Strozzi-Heckler, Richard. *The Leadership Dojo*. Berkeley, Calif.: North Atlantic Books, 2007.

Index

About the Author

Originally from Boston, Renée Gregorio has lived in New Mexico since 1985. She has a master's degree in creative writing from Antioch University, London. Renée is one of the founders of *The Taos Review,* one of New Mexico's foremost literary journals, as well as a founder of the publishing collective Tres Chicas Books. She's been dedicated to poem-making for the past four decades. She has also worked as a freelance literary editor, a proofreader and drafter for the state legislature, a writing teacher, and a somatic coach. Travel and her longtime practice of the Japanese martial art aikido inform her work's emergence as much as the land and spirit of northern New Mexico.

Renée's website, including a sampling of her poetry, can be viewed at **ReneeGregorio.com.** Her published volumes include the following:

The X Poems (Santa Fe, N.M.: X Press, 1992).
The Skins of Possible Lives (Taos, N.M.: Blinking Yellow Books, 1996).

The Storm That Tames Us (Albuquerque, N.M.: La Alameda Press, 1999).

Water Shed: Aikido Tanka (La Puebla, N.M.: Tres Chicas Books, 2004).

Road to the Cloud's House, with John Brandi (Santa Fe, N.M.: Palace Press, 2008).

Drenched (New York: Fish Drum, 2010).

Love & Death: Greatest Hits, with Joan Logghe and Miriam Sagan (La Puebla, N.M.: Tres Chicas Books, 2011).

Snow Falling on Snow (Glenview, Ill.: Glass Lyre Press, 2015).

Pa' Siempre: Cuba Poems, with John Brandi (La Puebla, N.M.: Tres Chicas Books, 2016).

What Is Given: Selected & New Poems (CD) (West Newbury, Mass.: On the Fringe Studios, 2020).

Abyss & Bridge (Denver, Colo.: 3: A Taos Press, 2021).